Teatime

Teatime
By The Tea Ambassador,
Aubrey Franklin

Frederick Fell Publishers, Inc.
New York, N.Y.

Copyright © 1981 by Aubrey Franklin

All rights reserved. No part of this work covered by the copyright may be reproduced or used in any form or by any means—graphic, electronic, or mechanical, including photocopying, recording, taping, or information storage and retrieval systems—without permission of the publisher.

For information address:
Frederick Fell Publishers, Inc.
386 Park Avenue South
New York, New York 10016

Library of Congress Catalog Card Number: 80-70953
International Standard Book Number: 0-8119-0414-8

MANUFACTURED IN THE UNITED STATES OF AMERICA
1 2 3 4 5 6 7 8 9 0

Published simultaneously in Canada by Fitzhenry and Whiteside Limited

Dedicated to "Frankie J."
and the many "spots of tea" we enjoyed together

Table of Contents

About the Author.......................... *xi*

Foreword: Steeped in Tradition .... *xvii*

History of Tea *1*
Stirrings in the Orient   *4*
The Japanese Tea Ceremony   *8*
Introduction of Tea into Europe   *10*
The Acceptance of Tea in England   *13*
Tea Comes to the U.S.A.   *14*
The Role of Tea in American History   *16*
The Great Tea Race of 1866   *24*

Tea-Totaling or Tea Customs Around the World 27
China 30
Japan 31
Russia 31
Turkey 32
Burma 32
North Thailand 32
Iran 33
Morocco 33
India and Sri Lanka (formerly Ceylon) 33
Australia 34
Canada 34
Great Britain and Ireland 35

Where Your Tea Comes From and How It Grows 37
Tea Goes Through Many Processes 42
Tea Has Many Grades as Well as Varieties 45
How Tea is Sold and How U.S. Government Tea Standards are Established 48
America Blends and Packages Its Tea 50

Why People Should Drink Tea 57
Thomas Sullivan "Had it in the Bag!" 61
How to Make the Perfect Cup of Tea 62
Looking for a Teapot 63
Kettles 64
Teacups 64

The Elevensey Cup	*65*
Infusers	*66*
Tea Storage	*67*
Drinking Your Tea	*67*
Tea for a Party? Here's the Answer— Fast and Foolproof!	*68*
Other Important Hints for Preparing Tea	*69*
Iced Tea	*70*
Why Not Blend Your Own Teas?	*75*

British Social Custom	*77*
The Beginnings of Informal Teatime	*79*

The Teas That Try One's Soul and Other Pretenders to the Throne	*83*
How to Order Tea in Restaurants and Hotels	*86*
The Tea That is Not a Tea—Herb Tea	*89*
Tea Pharmacy	*89*

Tan-tea-lizing Recipes	*91*
Hot Tea Recipes	*93*
Iced Tea Recipes	*98*
Spirited Teas	*103*
Recipes for Afternoon Tea	*118*
Recipes for High Tea or Light Supper	*125*
Savories	*132*
Cooking with Tea	*138*

Festivi-teas	*139*
Pies	*147*
Breads	*161*
Cakes, Buns, and Biscuits	*164*
Sweets	*177*
Recipe for Tea Leaf Reading	*192*
Conversion Tables	*196*

About the Author

If you can visualize a combination of Peter Ustinov, Terry-Thomas, David Niven, and Monty Woolley... you have just had the pleasure of meeting The Honorable Aubrey Franklin, the Tea Council's Ambassador. Because of his far-reaching reputation as a consultant to the food and beverage industry, the Tea Council, an organization whose principal function is to reacquaint the American public with this important beverage, chose Franklin as their Good Will Ambassador.

As he visits the various ex-Colonies, he gently educates the "barbarians" who habitually agitate the tea bag by dunking, sloshing, and squeezing it into tepid, or flat, hot water. With a mischievous twinkle in his eye and his typical tongue-in-cheek commentaries about "tea abusers," Franklin is determined to teach us Yanks how to become proper tea users. The Ambassador does not bear a grudge against us for sparking the War for Independence during the Boston Tea Party, but he does feel "it was a bit naughty of us to toss the precious cargo into cold water."

Franklin, now in his sixth year as Ambassador, recalls treasured moments of his youth. "When I was a young lad, teatime was that special hour for sharing stories and having a giggle or two with my family. These everyday gatherings, enhanced by the ritual of teatime, helped us to feel united. To be able to chat about the humorous and oftimes tremulous events of the day was not only cathartic, but enabled us to know and enjoy each other. This is what is needed today, a

time set aside for the specific purpose of sharing not only tea and its delicious accompaniments, but love. . . Instead of friends and families tuning out by immediately switching on the telly, start tuning in to one another again. Teatime is the perfect time and is a most delightfully exhilarating habit."

Franklin's personal history, although not as old as the tealeaf, is equally as romantic and intriguing. He was born and raised in London and Seaford, Sussex, where he went to school. During World War II, he served as an officer in the Queens Royal Fuseliers and with General Montgomery at El Alamein. While serving as both correspondent and photographer, he filmed *Desert Victory*. Later he was associated with 20th-Century Fox in England. The cosmopolitan Ambassador has lived under the most wondrous rooftops of the world—Paris, Brussels, Italy, India, and Hong Kong—his motto being, "Have teapot . . . will travel!"

This puckishly charming gentleman also is considered an international expert in wine and spirits. He was "Mr. Ambassador Scotch" in 1961 and represented the leading vineyards and distillers on a worldwide basis. Arriving in the United States in 1971, he decided to bring a bit of England to New York City. *The Great British Disaster* became one of the most well-known watering holes for glamorous film stars, journalists, media people, and all those seeking conviviality over "a pint or two." It actually was more like an unofficial club, and one never knew what "locals" might be arriving from some far-reaching corner of the earth for a bit of cheer.

Franklin opened it in his usual flamboyant way. Roger Moore (James Bond) called him on the "blower," or telephone, from England and speakers were placed around the pub. Franklin and 007 thereby officially established a British foothold in one of their former colonies. From that point on, it was, "Tally ho. . . . Bung ho. . . . And away we go!" With his ever present joie de vivre, Franklin became one of New York's favorite personalities. Libra is his astrological sign and he fits it to a "tea"—with creative flair and an unerring belief in whatever venture he embarks upon.

He was instrumental, for example, in introducing Irish Coffee to the United States in the early 1950's, as well as the "civilized British answer to that, which is Tea Saronno (Tea with Love). Its sensual, delicate flavor titillates the most discriminating palates. The combination of Amaretto liqueur tasting of almonds and apricots, plus freshly brewed tea topped by a generous mound of whipped cream, transforms even a simple dinner into elegant dining."

The increasing popularity of tea is attributed to the growing demand by the young people of today, under 35. They feel that a "tea break" gives them lasting gradual alertness during the day, as opposed to a jolt of pep. It is said that tea is soothing, rather than exciting and disturbing. For those of us who brown-bag it to work every day, or for singles who want tea for one, the Tea Ambassador suggests an 11:00 A.M. tea break with the *Elevensey Cup* (11:00 A.M. and 4:00 P.M. are traditional tea breaks in England). Actually, the *Elevensey Cup*, which was designed by Franklin, is a mug that has an accompanying lid. The lid should be set atop the mug allowing the tea bag to steep inside to its full flavor. The Honorable Aubrey Franklin's countenance is whimsically caricatured and grins impishly at you, as if to say, "There now . . . you've got a proper cuppa tea." (More information on this cup appears later on in this book.)

On a recent trip to London, Franklin rang up one of the directors of BSR Ltd., in Birmingham, England. (BSR is the major manufacturer of household, industrial, and commercial products in England, including an automatic tea machine.) As a result of Franklin's recognizing the need for this renowned machine in America, he met with BSR, which enthusiastically advised him to "press on, old chap!"

BSR's *Teasmade* has been a household must for every home in England since 1936. Franklin says, "With the *Teasmade*, the water is brought just to the boiling point in a chrome-on-copper kettle and transferred automatically to the heat-retaining ceramic teapot. Then it's merely a matter of waiting three to five minutes for the tea to brew to your taste. Tea bags or loose tea leaves work equally as well."

Teasmade has been designed for modern living; its futuristic design is sleek, streamlined, and enhances any part of your home or apartment. Most Britishers place it by their bedside, thereby enabling them to just reach over and presto, almost magically, have breakfast in bed! Aside from *Teasmade* being luxuriously functional—at the flick of a switch, it's a bedside lamp; at a glance, it's the perfect time keeper (with luminous hands); and at the twist of a knob, it's your most reliable alarm clock—it makes tea immediately, in addition to hot chocolate, coffee, broth, etc. *Teasmade* is now available in the United States for the first time, its initial presentation was just before Christmas, 1979.

The Honorable Aubrey Franklin, apart from his other talents, has a poetic side to his nature. This is gleefully dedicated to tea:

THE PERFECT CUPPA TEA

I'm just a very simple man,
Who likes a "perfect cuppa tea."
Brewed tenderly . . . properly . . .
A heavenly blend
That puts an end
To everyday anxiety.
So come fill your cup,
And lift your soul and spirits up.

Foreword

Steeped in Tradition

Sit down with a relaxing cup of tea and let your mind wander. You might find yourself sailing a romantic clipper ship at the height of the China tea trade. Or dumping boxes of the leaves to the fish in Boston harbor. Or wearing a kimono at a formal Japanese tea ceremony. Or solving a British murder mystery over high tea, surrounded by silver trays of scones, crumpets, cakes, and finger sandwiches.

Tea is rich in tradition, and part of that tradition is stopping for a bit and letting the frantic world go on without you while you relax, and perhaps daydream. The British, of course, are masters of the art. British soldiers literally called World War II to a halt every afternoon at 4:00, while they took their tea. It drove the American soldiers up the wall at first, but given time, they, too, learned to enjoy the tradition. Today, more and more Americans are finding tea the cup that soothes.

Teatime

History of Tea

The best guess is that tea drinking began in southwest China about 4000 years ago. The Amoy Chinese called the potion *T'se* (pronounced tay), whereas the Canton Chinese referred to it as *Ch'a* (pronounced chah). As the Chinese exported tea to Java and—courtesy of the Dutch—ultimately to Europe and North America, it became known as "tay." With its popularity, the name changed to "tee" or "tea." But "chah" was the term for the tea leaves, compressed with oxblood into bricks that were transported via the great Asian caravan routes to Russia, India, and Persia. As a matter of fact, it's not unusual in Great Britain today to hear the term "How about a cup of chah?", particularly among the cockneys.

Stirrings in the Orient

Life was very simple and man had only a glimmering of his present day knowledge when the Chinese Emperor Shen Nung knelt before a fire, boiling water. Called the "Divine Healer," the wise Emperor always boiled water before drinking it. Nobody knew the causes of illnesses, but Shen Nung had observed that people who boiled their drinking water had better health.

Shen Nung's servants had made the fire from the branches of a nearby tree. As the water began to boil, some of the topmost leaves of the branches were blown into the pot.

"What a delightful aroma!" exclaimed the Emperor as the fragrance of tea floated into the air for the first time. He sipped the steaming liquid. "Ah!" And what a flavor!" That, as the Chinese will tell you, is how tea was discovered around 2737 B.C.

The people of Japan have their own story about the origin of tea as a drink. According to their legend, about 1900 years ago a saintly Buddhist priest named Darma wanted to prove his faith. He decided to do so by spending seven years without sleep, thinking only of Buddha. For five years, day and night, Darma thought of Buddha. Then one day, to his dismay, he found himself falling asleep. Darma fought to keep his eyes open. In desperation, he snatched a handful of leaves from a nearby bush and chewed them. Maybe they would keep him awake! The leaves, of course, were leaves from a tea bush. Darma felt refreshed and

Teatime

awake after chewing them. With their help, he was able to complete his seven years of meditation on Buddha uninterrupted by sleep.

While all history until the seventh century B.C. remains legend, it may be safe to say that the holy men traveling between China and its border regions introduced tea, since tea grows wild in these areas of India, Burma, Tibet, and China. Before the seventh century, it is also impossible to tell whether the Chinese symbols referred to tea or to the herb, sow thistle. The symbols vary only slightly.

In 206 A.D., during the Han period, a restoration began and books were rewritten. Therefore, since previous history was based on religious beliefs rather than fact, the new books were taken as gospel. Shen Nung was given his credibility by the Han scholars, since it suited their thoughts on the way things might have been. At the end of the third century and the dissolution of the Han Empire, tea drinking became widespread. An ancient dictionary, the *Erh Ya*, attributed to the Duke of Chou (eighth century B.C.) was annotated in 350 A.D. by Kuo P'o, a Chinese scholar who conceivably added the definition of tea. A fifth-century dictionary described tea as a pleasant beverage and gave a description on how to make it into a drink. Around this period, tea became an export. Its importance was reflected by the tea tax levied in 793.

The T'ang Dynasty reigned from 618-907, bringing to China a new love for the arts, music, culture, and a greater awareness for their produce.

At this time, the tea merchants commissioned Lu

Yu, an artist who reflected the spirit of Chinese culture, to write a book on tea that would promote the industry. The resulting masterwork, the *Ch'a Ching*, a three-volume, ten-part series on tea drinking and its history, varieties, and preparation, bestowed upon Lu Yu the stature of pre-eminence among the Chinese merchants. Lu Yu, however, rejected their attention and instead retired to the mountains, where he lived in solitude for the rest of his life. Nevertheless, Lu Yu was the tea connoisseur who established the standards and created a format for judging the quality of tea. He credited those with knowledge of tea as "connoisseurs of an inferior order"—all others were "ordinary connoisseurs."

Whipped tea—powdered leaves that were whipped in hot water with a bamboo whisk—became popular during the Sung period (930-1280). Tea also became a collector's item, with its utensils assuming the value of art and the art of tea drinking emerging as a social grace. Public tea houses were built, and Buddhists added tea drinking to their rites. As the various dynasties changed, so did the importance of tea drinking. Tea disappeared from the Imperial Court during the Mongol reign 1271-1294); Marco Polo, who resided at court during that time, never mentioned tea. Then, when the Ming Dynasty took over (1368-1644), tea became a way of life for all classes.

During this time a fairly complex system of banking had developed in the populated centers, although minted money was distrusted. Instead, tea was frequently used for barter—the further it was shipped, the higher the price. To transport the tea,

Teatime

leaves were compressed into "bricks," fired, and later broken into small pieces that were made into a drink often flavored with jasmine blossoms, ginger, oranges, or onions. (Flavored teas made from wild, as opposed to cultivated, leaves had been known for at least 1500 years throughout Southeast Asia.)

While the Chinese turned tea drinking into an art, in Japan it took on the appearance of a mystical ceremony. The preparation of tea in both China and Japan is regarded as a symbolic bond with the elements of nature. The boiling water in China relates to the mountain mists, rippling waters, and floating clouds, while the Zen Buddhist priests in Japan portrayed three stages of heating water. First, the bubbles were related to the eyes of fish, followed by falling beads of crystal, and finally, the boiling of water becomes the seething waves of the seas.

Tea journeyed to Japan with the Japanese priests who introduced Buddhism to the Japanese; the tea form of the Sung Dynasty was the one used in Japan. The Japanese Tea Ceremony had its beginning in 1477. The priest Okakura called the culture of tea, "a moral geometry in that it puts man in his proper place in the universe . . . and, accordingly, man must go outside himself in order to regard life as a spectator . . ." With these concepts in mind, the tea ceremony becomes a dedication of man's humility and his desire to live in harmony with himself and his fellow man.

The Japanese Tea Ceremony

The tea ceremony took much of its purpose and philosophy from Zen religion because the first tea masters were priests, who had greatly influenced Japanese culture and social customs. The priests taught that enlightenment could only be reached through Zen meditation, and the tea ceremony became a means of disciplining one's mind. Sen-no Rikyu is credited with setting down the rules for the tea ceremony in 1584, and making some dramatic changes in methods of serving tea and also in the utensils used.

Ultimately, others felt that Rikyu had become too powerful a figure. While he challenged those who regarded the tea ceremony as a profit-making venture, he himself was accused of selling tea articles, which was considered a heinous crime. Moreover, Rikyu infuriated Hideyoshi, his master, when he placed a statue of himself on one of the temple gates. Ordered to commit suicide, Rikyu did so on January 28, 1591, to the satisfaction of his enemies.

The Japanese Tea Ceremony is a rite of selection, for each guest is carefully chosen by the host. There never are more than five guests, who all must be compatible among themselves and with the host. They dress judiciously for the ceremony, avoiding ostentatious apparel. Nothing must intrude upon the ritual.

Upon arrival, the guests congregate in the waiting room, where they inspect the articles that have been arranged there. Soon the host arrives. He opens the sliding door, stands in the doorway, bows to his guests, and then silently returns to the tea room. The guests follow him out of the waiting room and proceed down a garden path. En route to the tea room, they are expected to meditate upon nature. As they pass a water-filled stone basin, they wash themselves in accordance with purification rites. Then, entering the tea room through a low door, each guest kneels in front of a small alcove to inspect the hanging scroll that later is replaced by a floral arrangement. Next, they admire the small incense holder on a side shelf.

Sometimes a meal is served, entirely by the host, to the guests, who must eat everything. Upon finishing, the guests put their empty dishes and bowls on separate trays, which the host removes one by one. The guests return to the waiting room, where they stay until they hear the sound of a gong, signaling the time for the ceremonial tea. As they return, they observe that the scroll in the alcove has been replaced by a flower arrangement.

The fresh-water vessel (*mizusashi*) and the tea caddy (*cha-ire*) are in place. The guests sit; the host enters with the tea bowl, whisk (*ohasen*), cloth (*chakin*), and teaspoon (*cha-shaku*). He sets them down, leaves, and then returns with the receptacle for waste water (*koboshi*), the dipper (*hishaku*), and the stand for the dipper and kettle cover (*fataoki*).

Water boils in the kettle over the charcoal hearth as the guests listen to the sound and comment on the kettle. Next, the tea is prepared: three spoonsful of tea are placed in the bowl, which is then filled with hot water. The dipper used in this process is returned to the kettle into which any excess water is poured; both instruments are then set aside.

The host stirs the tea with the whisk until it becomes foamy. The principal guest then receives the tea bowl, bows to the other guests, and sips the tea. He compliments the host, takes another sip, and passes the bowl to the next person. The last guest in the circle finishes the tea. The bowl, tea caddy, and spoon are then passed around for all the guests to admire.

The tea ceremony just described has so evolved from the tenets set forth by Rikyu. Among his directions, in a list of seven rules, is that participants should have not only clean faces and hands, but also clean hearts. Host and guests are forbidden, too, to speak of wordly matters such as politics, nor may they flatter one another by "word or deed." A guest has the option to leave if the host's poverty precludes the presence of tea and other necessities for the ceremony, or if the edibles are tasteless, "or even if the trees and rocks do not please him." Normally, though, the ceremony was expected to last not longer than two hours (Japanese) to four hours (European) time.

Introduction of Tea into Europe

Tea was unknown to the Europeans until 1559, when news of the herb was published in Venice. Yet not until 1610, in the midst of a seagoing rivalry between Holland and Portugal, did tea actually come to Europe.

After the discovery by Vasco da Gama in 1497 of an all-sea route to the Indies via the Cape of Good Hope, the Portuguese founded a base of operations in the Malay Peninsula. They pushed on to China in 1516, and by 1540 entered Japan. The Portuguese convinced the initially hostile Chinese that they had come to barter and trade, not invade. Commerce began with Japan as well, but there is no record at this point of any transactions involving tea.

Jesuit missionaries, however, who were early visitors to both countries, sent reports of tea to Europe. Father Gaspar da Cruz, a Portuguese, reported his findings in 1560. Soon further news of tea reached Italy in 1565 through correspondence from Father Louis Almeida, a missionary to Japan. Descriptions of tea were received by Russia in 1567, were again noted in an Italian work in 1588, and were spreading in France around the early- to mid-seventeenth century.

Until 1596, the Portuguese had monopolized the sea trade to the Orient. By closing their ports to Dutch commerce in 1595, they forced the Dutch to map their own direct route to the Indies, where they formed the East India Company. In 1607, the Dutch transported some tea from Macao to Java, the first recorded instance of any transport of tea by a European country stationed in the East. Three years later, the Dutch began shipping tea to Europe.

In 1611, the Dutch secured trading privileges with Japan. The Portuguese missionaries who had settled in Japan, it happens, had so offended that country by their interference in affairs of state that the Japanese accepted Dutch assistance in ousting the Portuguese. For their efforts, the Dutch were allowed to remain, but were forced to reside inside stone walls on an island in the harbor of Nagasaki. Under these humiliating circumstances, Dutch tea trade with Japan came to a halt.

Instead, the Dutch turned to China for supplies. At the turn of the seventeenth century, the Dutch had acquired almost complete control of the spice trade in the Indies. Gradually, though, the English East India Company was gathering strength in the East. By 1611, the English had established factories in India, thus moving in on the Dutch dominance of trade.

The Dutch, however, were demanding that the English leave and, in fact, the first teas to reach England arrived on Dutch ships. A military defeat by Dutch forces, known as the Massacre of Amboyna (1623), sent the English to the refuge of mainland India and adjoining countries. Shipments of tea by the English did not start in earnest until 1669, when the English East India Company imported 143½ pounds from Bantam, in Java. The venture marked the beginning of a shipping business that would eventually surpass that of the rival Dutch and Portuguese.

Meanwhile, through the auspices of a Chinese embassy, the first shipment of tea to the Russian court in Moscow arrived in 1618. As the overland journey had taken eighteen months, the condition of the tea did not impress the Russians. Some fifteen years later, it is believed, tea first appeared in Paris. There it met with considerable opposition, most particularly among physicians. When some doctors hailed the beverage as a panacea, the resulting uproar in French medical circles escalated so that no other physicians would come out in favor of tea.

While Russia, Eastern Europe, and France disdained tea drinking at this stage, the upper classes at the Hague were beginning to adopt tea as a fashionable beverage around 1640. About ten years later, Holland introduced tea to Germany, where, by 1657, it had become a staple trade item. Yet, there was adverse reaction in Germany: the Jesuit Martino Martini claimed that the Chinese were withered-looking and that tea was the cause.

The use of tea had spread also in the Scandinavian countries. In all likelihood, they had become familiar with tea both through the Danes, who began to participate in the Indian trade in 1616, and the Dutch. And in Holland, between 1660 and 1680, a broader acceptance of tea had developed, filtering first to the homes of the gentry, then to the houses of the bourgeoisie and the poor.

The Acceptance of Tea in England

Tea drinking came to be enjoyed by everyone through its appearance in the London coffee houses of the seventeenth century, where it was served alongside coffee, chocolate, and sherbert. The ladies of England, on the other hand, accepted tea as a fashionable drink during the era of Catherine of Braganza, the Portuguese princess and tea enthusiast whom Charles II married in 1662. In the year of her marriage, English poet Edmund Waller (1606–87) wrote an ode to tea in honor of the birthday of Queen

Catherine, which began: "Venus her myrtle, Phoebus has his bays; / Tea both excels, which she vouchsafes to praise."

A few years earlier, in 1658, the *Sultaness Head Coffee House*, one of the first such places to offer tea as part of its menu, placed a notice advertising the drink in the newspaper *Mercurius Politicus*: "That excellent and by all Physitians approved China drink, called by the Chineans Tcha, by other Nations Tay, aliea Tee, is sold at the Sultaness Head Cophee House in Sweetings Rents, by the Royal Exchange, London." All through the rest of the seventeenth century and most of the eighteenth, the sale of tea increased in the London coffee houses. These "penny universities," as they were sometimes known—great schools of conversation at an admission cost of a penny—sold a dish of tea or coffee for twopence, which also covered the price of newspapers and lights.

The first establishment specializing in the serving of tea, the *Golden Lyon*, was opened by Thomas Twining in 1717. Unlike the coffee houses of the period, which were frequented by men only, this first tea shop in England was visited by both sexes.

Tea Comes to the U.S.A.

Tea is so much a part of our life in the United States today that it is hard to imagine a time when it was not known in American homes. Yet those courageous men and women who crossed the cold and turbulent Atlantic to settle in this country had no tea

Teatime

to comfort and cheer them. Neither was there any tea—nor coffee for that matter—served at that first Thanksgiving feast in November of 1621 because tea and coffee were not known here, or even in Europe, in the early 1600's.

No one knows when tea was first brought to this country. It is believed that ships plying between the Dutch colony of New Amsterdam and its mother country, Holland, carried the first tea to this country about 1650. The food-loving burghers of New Amsterdam were probably the first people in America to try the new beverage that was then so popular in Europe.

Tea quickly became fashionable in New Amsterdam despite the fact that it cost from thirty to fifty dollars a pound. The socially correct lady of that day not only served tea, but also brewed several kinds of tea in different pots to suit the tastes of her guests. Sometimes, she offered saffron or peach leaves for flavoring. (Milk, used with tea, was not known until later.) Records of the period show she was proud of her tea table, teapots, sugar bowl, silver spoons, and tea strainer. In Massachusetts, the English colonists began to use tea to a limited extent, probably as early as 1670.

When tea was first brought here, few people knew how to prepare it. Considering what they did with the little dried leaves, it is a wonder that tea ever became popular. In Salem, Massachusetts, tea leaves were boiled until a bitter brew resulted, which the colonists drank without milk or sugar. Then they salted the leaves and ate them with butter.

After New Amsterdam passed into the hands of the English in 1674 and became New York, it adopted English customs and manners. Tea gardens became popular and people brought water for making tea from special pumps. Ladies went to parties, each carrying her own teacup, saucer, and spoon. The cups were fashioned of the most delicate china and were so small that they held as little as a common wineglass.

As for furniture, the first record of a tea table made in America was in 1705. Tea was drunk with meals and at special parties; the custom of afternoon tea was not known. It was not until years later that people began to serve afternoon tea to tide over the long wait between the noonday and evening meals.

Since the first pound of tea arrived in the United States over 300 years ago, the tea industry has grown enormously. It now employs many thousands of people and represents millions of dollars. Americans now drink an average of around forty-six billion servings of tea each year. About thirty-seven billion of these are iced tea. Over 200 million pounds of tea are imported into the United States annually.

The Role of Tea in American History

In 1763, at the close of the Seven Years' War, England had established both its naval supremacy and its dominance in North America. George III, in stating that the war had been waged in defense of the colonies, determined that they should be taxed for part of the cost of the British troops who had secured that defense. The ministry of George Grenville therefore passed the Stamp Act of 1765, which imposed taxes on tea and other articles used by the colonists.

Protests arose immediately, not only in America, but also among English opponents of the Grenville ministry. Taking the position that the British Parliament had no right to tax the Americans without the consent of their colonial assemblies, William Pitt led the opposition at home. Although the government repealed the act the next year, it asserted by the Declaratory Act its supreme right to set taxes and laws for the colonies. In 1767, Parliament passed Charles Townshend's Act of Trade and Revenue, which also laid duties on tea and other articles.

Now the colonists refused to import any items from England, whose merchants were beginning to feel the loss of their lucrative markets. Parliament then repealed every tax except a duty of threepence per pound on tea. The colonists still refused to pay it and instead engaged in a brisk business of smuggled tea from Holland. The smuggling venture was a key aspect of this early history; many farmers left their fields to get into that profitable business.

Meanwhile, the English East India Company panicked at these trade defections and the resulting tea surplus, so it appealed to Parliament for assistance. Prime Minister Lord North passed the Tea Act of 1773, which ultimately led to the Boston Tea Party. By this act, the East India Company was authorized to send its teas directly to the colonies, thus eliminating the profits of both the middlemen and the American importers. Until that time, English jobbers had purchased tea from the East India Company and then resold and shipped it to the colonial merchants.

The Act of 1773 also stipulated that the East India Company be allowed to rescind the full amount of the 100 percent English duty when the teas where shipped out of England, which left only the threepenny tax to be collected by colonial customs officials. It was felt that this plan would undercut the Dutch even as it gave the colonists lower-priced teas than those available in England. Yet the American colonists, on principle, refused the bargain-priced tea on account of the threepence-per-pound tax.

The East India Company proceeded to carry out these adjustments by appointing special agents to receive the tea on consignment, upon payment of the duty, in Boston, New York, Philadelphia, and Charleston. At the same time, resentment to the Tea Act, and to all events that had preceded it, had been building up in America. The most noted form of protest took shape in the groups called the Sons of Liberty. In addition, many women's groups in Boston, Hartford, and other American cities pledged themselves not to drink tea. In some parts of Massachusetts, it was impossible to obtain tea without a permit, which usually was issued only for a person who was critically ill. Meanwhile, substitutes such as roots, bark, flowers, and leaves were being boiled and consumed by colonists everywhere.

As protests continued to mount, letters to England warned of American anger over its actions, but to no avail. Over here, the colonial press picked up the fight and explained the manner in which the duty was to be collected: "On a certificate of its being landed here, the tribute says is, by agreement, to be paid to London. The landing is, therefore, the point in view." With the landing as the issue, the merchants, backed by various patriotic groups such as the Sons of Liberty, decided that the tea should not land.

Philadelphia led the resistance to English authority and circulated a handbill with the heading, "United we stand, divided we fall," which signaled that all colonists should resist the invasion of their rights. On October 18, 1773, a meeting held at the State House declared that the tax was an unwarranted duty and that any person attempting to unload or sell English tea was engaging in treason. Eight days later, a similar mass meeting was held in New York at City Hall. The New York members, however, announced that customs officials would take custody of arriving tea shipments, which prompted much resentment from many quarters. The Sons of Liberty warned all storekeepers against holding the tea, declaring, as had the Philadelphians, that those who bought or sold it would be considered traitors.

Nearly every colony had its own branch of the Sons of Liberty, which controlled public policy throughout the events that led to the tea revolt. The organization served its own warrants, made arrests, arranged slates for elections, and planned celebrations. In Boston, meetings were held with great secrecy in various parts of the city. While the governor of Massachusetts tried to use his authority to have the tea unloaded, the Sons of Liberty proved too numerous and too alert.

On Sunday, November 28, 1773, the *Dartmouth*,

commanded by Captain Hall, was the first tea ship to arrive in Boston since the protests against the tax began. Aboard the ship was a cargo of 80 whole and 34 half chests of tea. The *Beaver* and the *Bedford*, manned by Captains Bruce and Coffin, arrived later. The ships remained in the harbor during a series of unsuccessful negotiations.

In the darkness of night on December 16, knots of Bostonians milled about the harbor. "Who knows," merchant John Rowe remarked, "how tea will mix with salt water?" With those words, from twenty to ninety citizens, accompanying their Indian disguises with war-whoops, boarded the ships, forced open the tea chests with hatchets and axes, and dumped the tea into the harbor. Similar "tea parties" followed in rapid succession from the shores of New Jersey to Charleston Bay.

Greenwich A tea ship docked unexpectedly in Greenwich, New Jersey, on December 12, 1773. Its intended destination had been Philadelphia, but its cargo was stored instead in the cellar of a house belonging to a Greenwich royalist. Word arrived from Philadelphia that the shipment had not landed there, so on December 22, young men from Greenwich and neighboring towns dressed as Indians and burned the tea in the middle of Market Square.

Charleston Around the same time, the ship *London*, carrying a consignment of the East India Company's tea, arrived at Charleston, South Carolina. The town's citizens met and decided that until the tax was

abolished, the tea should not be unloaded. Since the local law stated that the cargo would revert to the collector of customs after twenty days, they seized it by force and stored it in damp vaults, where it quickly spoiled. Subsequent arrivals of tea also were seized and stored in dampness, but when seven more chests of tea aboard the *Britannia Ball* arrived on November 3, 1774, the Charlestonians decided to hold a "tea party." The owners, fearing that their ship, as well as the cargo, would be burned, joined the citizens in destroying the chests and dumping their contents overboard. A similar incident occurred soon afterwards in Georgetown, South Carolina; disguises were not used at either demonstration.

Philadelphia On Christmas Day, 1773, Philadelphians learned that a tea ship was proceeding toward the city, and a committee was on hand for the ship's arrival at Gloucester Point the next day. It invited her commander, Captain Ayres, to come ashore to determine the mood of the people; the crowd that gathered to meet him included a number of citizens bearing placards that requested he be tarred and feathered. On December 27, the largest crowd ever assembled in the town held a meeting with Captain Ayres in the square outside the State House. The assemblage resolved that the tea could not be landed; that the captain could not report his vessel at the Custom House; that the captain leave immediately, and that a committee of gentlemen be appointed to see that he do so. Captain Ayres pledged to follow orders and departed to London with the tea.

New York The *Nancy* left London with a tea cargo in September, 1773. She was destined for New York, but storms drove the ship off course to Antigua, in the British West Indies. On April 18, 1774, she finally reached New York, where her Captain Lockyear was met by fifteen Sons of Liberty and her small boats were padlocked to prevent desertion by the crew that would have to steer the ship back to London. On April 22, the tea ship *London*, commanded by Captain Chambers, also arrived in New York, although the local Vigilance Committee refused to allow the *London* to dock. Chambers at first denied that tea was aboard and so was allowed to land. The Vigilance Committee, it happens, was not convinced and upon boarding the ship received the captain's admission that he had eighteen chests of tea on hand for his personal use. The crowd that had been on the dock swarmed aboard, broke open the chests, and threw away the contents. Chambers, threatened with violence, managed to board the *Nancy*, which departed the next morning to the enthusiasm of celebrating citizens congregated at the foot of Wall Street, and to the sounds of a band playing the English national anthem.

Annapolis On October 14, 1774, the *Peggy Stewart* approached Annapolis with a 2000-pound cargo of tea. Citizens immediately resolved not to permit the tea to land, while the fate of the cargo was postponed for five days. At the meeting on October 19, people were angered that Anthony Stewart, the ship's owner and a resident of Annapolis, had already defeated their principles by having paid duty on the tea. Preparations for lynching Stewart were begun, but the alarmed merchant apologized to the crowd and offered to bring the tea ashore and burn it. His offer failed to placate the crowd, however, which erected a gallows in front of his house and gave him an option: swing by the neck or put fire to his ship. He chose the latter; shortly thereafter, he returned to his native Scotland.

Edenton Fifty-one women in Edenton, North Carolina, drew up a paper on October 25, 1774, that condemned the tea tax. They then signed their names to the document and sent it to *The Morning Chronicle and London Advertiser.* Its publication on January 16, 1775, created an uproar in England; it read in part:

> The provincial deputies of North Carolina, having resolved not to drink any more tea, nor wear any more British cloth, and many ladies of this province have determined to give a memorable proof of their patriotism, and have accordingly entered into the following honourable and spirited association. I send it to you to show your fair countrywomen, how zealously and faithfully American ladies follow the laudable example of their husbands, and what opposition your matchless ministers may expect to receive from a people, thus firmly united against them.

The Great Tea Race of 1866

By the mid-nineteenth century, the hostilities between the nascent American nation and England had been transformed to a competitive struggle between two seafaring giants. It was the era of the clipper ships: with all sails set, scudding along under a brisk breeze, these ships were a thrilling sight.

The clippers were specifically designed for the speedy transport of tea; ships raced from China to London or to New York for prizes of thousands of dollars. The most famous of these races started on May 26, 1866, from the Pagody anchorage in the Min River below Foochow, and ended 99 days later in the London docks.

The competition truly began, however, in the offices of the ships' agents and in the warehouses of the Chinese merchants, for monetary rewards were to be had on the winning ship. Favorites for the race, therefore, got the first chests and were first to complete loading.

Although the *Ariel* finished loading first, she made a false start and put to anchor before the tide had fallen. *Fiery Cross* passed her and set out to sea, while *Serica* and *Taeping* followed. All ships had left the harbor by the seventh of June.

Despite her initial problems, the *Ariel* was the first to arrive in London on September 6, ten minutes before *Taeping*. The two crews agreed to call it a draw and split the premium. Who realized then that this exhilarating race among these evenly matched clippers signaled the beginning of the end—the Suez Canal opened its channels to the steamer ships in 1869, thus consigning the tea clippers to history.

Tea-Totaling or Tea Customs Around the World

As tea holds the good fortune of being the second-largest consumer beverage in the world (water being number one), it would seem that there is much pleasure to gain in joining me in "tea-sing" you around the world as to everybody's cup of tea.

The Chinese lead is no surprise, followed by the British and the Irish, who are always chanting, "How about a cup of Rosey Lee [tea]?" In Burma, believe it or not, tea is consumed as a pickled relish, while in North Africa, a glass of mint tea is the introduction to any business dealings. Let's travel now in some detail:

China

It goes without saying, that the Chinese who introduced it are the world's most avid tea drinkers. They drink tea all day. The custom of serving tea to guests is said to go back to the Sung Dynasty; whatever the occasion, the rulers served tea at court.

Travelers to China today will find in their hotel rooms a small bag of green tea, a thermos bottle with hot water, and covered glasses. On the trains, next to your seat, there's a wooden rack with glasses and a fresh supply of tea leaves. The train attendant walks up and down the aisle filling or refilling your glass with hot water. Naturally, teahouses are all over the country. It's the custom to receive two cups, a big one for brewing and a very small one for drinking. According to Yuen-Ren Chao, the importance of the teahouse has a double meaning: "Shang Ch'a Kuan'r," when interpreted, means "to go to the teahouse" or "having a dispute arbitrated at a teahouse."

Today, there are tea bricks available in the United States that are produced by the same method employed by the Chinese ancients when they devised a more efficient method of transporting their valued commodity by camel trains to Mongolia and Tibet. The bricks also were used as a medium of exchange. (The Tibetan enjoyed his brick of tea by boiling it with yak butter in a large cauldron.) Should you desire to buy and prepare brick tea yourself, pulverize one teaspoon of tea per cup. Pour boiling water over the tea, stir, and let settle.

Japan

Japan has the most colorful history as far as tea drinking goes. They use a finely powdered green tea (Mattcha), which is whisked with hot water into a thick froth. The Zen masters brought this form of tea to Japan and, through the ages, created a ritual around its preparation and serving. (See "The Japanese Tea Ceremony.")

Russia

The Russians have been ardent tea drinkers since the 1800's. Their favorite tea is Smoky Lapsang, which is black and strong and consumed hot, in glasses with sugar and lemon. (The use of tea glasses is traditional throughout Russia, North Africa, and the Middle East.)

The samovar, which in Russian means "self-boiler," is the dream of most Russians to own. This unique accessory goes back 200 years, when the Tartars called it *Sanabar*, or "tea urn." The samovar has a small stove that is usually heated with charcoal. Up to forty cups of water can be held in the water chamber; the top vent, or crown, holds the teapot with dark and strong tea. The purpose is to drain tea-colored brew from the teapot by refilling it time and again from the samovar. Lemon, preserves, or sugar may be stirred into the tea. It's the custom that cubes of sugar are placed in the mouth, and the tea sucked through the teeth. Today, the samovar is made of nickel and chrome and is not confined to its traditional uses. It can make hot and cold prepared punches, or other mixed drinks; it's not unusual to find tea laced with rum or any of the fruit brandies. If you buy a samovar, you can receive much pleasure using it at parties.

Turkey

Turkey also uses a samovar to serve tea; colorful street vendors dispense of the beverage in this manner. Its popularity has grown with successful efforts by the government to encourage the Turkish people to give up coffee and drink more tea, since it is grown locally.

Burma

The Burmese boil fresh tea leaves until soft and then roll, cool, and jam them them into a piece of bamboo. The bamboo is plugged with guava leaves and buried until the tea ferments. Then the tea, mixed with oil, garlic, and dried fish, is eaten as a delicacy. It is called *letpet*.

North Thailand

A wild tea, called *miang*, is gathered in the forests, steamed, and fermented. Then it is mixed with salt and flavorings such as garlic and pork fat. The result is chewed as a stimulant.

Iran

Tea is the national drink. Iranian tea houses serve tea in small glasses with lumps of sugar, through which the tea is sipped. Spoons are not used, unless requested.

Morocco

Green tea is the favored drink here, where it is mixed with dried mint and sugar. As you enter a store, the merchant immediately serves you a cup of tea, which, of course, gives him more time to try to sell his goods.

India and Sri Lanka (formerly Ceylon)

India and Sri Lanka follow the British fashion of tea drinking, since the British introduced tea cultivation to them. The tea shop is the center of social activity in India, where tourists or workers can rest from the heat of the day. Indians join the occupied tables and strike up conversations with strangers as if they were friends, unlike the American custom, in which everyone looks for the unoccupied tables. In India, even the poor start their day with a cup of tea, filled with sugar and buffalo milk; it may be the only food they get all day. If a person is too poor to pay the two cents a cup, someone will donate the cost or the tea shop will give it on the house.

Australia

The famous "Waltzing Mathilda" song talks of "billy boil'd," referring to "billy tea," which is boiled in a tin can over an open fire. It is the bushman's way of drinking tea: he throws a handful of tea leaves into a billy that is full of water and puts it over the fire to boil. After drinking his morning tea, he leaves the billy simmering all day while he is gone. Then, when he returns that evening, he has some more billy tea—a bit strong, I must say. Throughout the rest of Australia, most tea is consumed as the British would, with milk and sugar to taste.

Canada

In 1715, the Hudson Bay Company introduced tea to Canada. Since then, tea has become the national beverage of that country. It's interesting to note that the tea varies according to the region: in Quebec, it's "make mine green," while the Canadian Eskimos, who love tea most of all, drink it strong and sweet, and enjoy chewing the leaves.

Great Britain and Ireland

One thing the British and the Irish do have in common—they both consume the largest amount of tea per year, about ten pounds per person. The Irish drink tea from breakfast to midnight and like it strong, almost like mud. Irish Breakfast tea is designed so the flavor comes through, even with milk. In Great Britain, tea is a way of life and afternoon tea is an institution not to be trifled with. No wonder, then, that the United Kingdom imports half the world's tea and that the most used phrase in the British Isles is "Put the kettle on" or "Tea's-up!"

Where Your Tea Comes from and How It Grows

Those little dried leaves you held in your hand at the beginning of our story grew on a bush halfway around the world from the U.S.A. For tea, as you know it, is the dried leaf of an evergreen plant, related to the camellia family, which grows wild where longitude 100 degrees east crosses the Tropic of Cancer at the meeting place of Tibet, India, China, and Burma.

About seventy percent of the tea America drinks each year comes from India, Indonesia, Sri Lanka, Kenya, Malawi, and Tanzania. Other major producing countries are China, Formosa, Iran, Japan, Turkey, Bangladesh, the U.S.S.R., and several South American countries. If you look at a map you will see that these countries are all in tropical or subtropical climates. Tea plants, which grow to a height of thirty feet, flourish where it is warm and where a great deal of rain falls. Paradoxically, while the plant grows most luxuriantly in the heat, teas grown in cooler altitudes of 3000 to 7000 feet are the finest quality produced. This slower growth at higher altitudes adds to the flavor of tea, but the yield is smaller, making this high grown tea rarer and more expensive. Many of the tea gardens of India, Sri Lanka, and Kenya, from which come some of the world's finest teas, are more than 6000 feet high.

Tea can be grown at all elevations from sea level to over 6000 feet. Since it is a jungle plant, it grows best in jungle soils. Tea is a hardy plant, which will take much punishment from both climate and soil. It demands a great deal of rain yet refuses to grow in swampy land. It will grow in soil ranging from light sands to stiffest clays, and has even been known to grow on land too poor for any other crop.

Tea is usually grown from seeds obtained by allowing certain plants to grow unchecked until they become trees fifteen or twenty feet high. Small, white, sweet-smelling flowers, not unlike apple blossoms, cover the seed trees in bloom time. The seeds from these flowers are much like a hazel nut in size and appearance.

At planting time, the seeds are laid out six inches apart. When the young plants are six to eighteen months old they are ready for removal to the tea garden. Approximately 3000 plants to one acre are set out about four feet apart.

Early in its growth, the young plant is cut back or pruned to encourage the main stem to grow more side branches. Constant cutting keeps the bush from

growing into the tree nature intended. Each bush is kept cut to about three or four feet in height and width so that the harvesters or pluckers can reach all its leaves.

After the tea plant has been transplanted and pruned, several years pass before it is ready to yield choice leaves. At lower elevations the young plants produce some harvest in three years. In the hills it may take as long as five years before a plant can produce sprouting new leaves, called "flushes," from which tea is produced.

A tea plantation or "estate" is carefully planned according to the slope or contour of the land. Terraces or long slopes help to prevent soil erosion. Trees are placed to shade the tea plants and to serve as windbreakers from monsoons or seasonal winds.

Sometimes ropeways or wire "shoots" similar to ski-tows are stretched from distant hilltops on which tea is growing to the buildings where tea is processed. The ropeways carry the freshly plucked leaves in sacks from the fields down to the tea factory.

Tea Goes Through Many Processes

According to Chinese philosopher Ts'ai Hsiang, "The essence of the enjoyment of tea lies in the appreciation of its color, fragrance, and flavor."

Ts'ai Hsiang's words are as true today as when he wrote them nearly a thousand years ago. Those are the criteria by which today's tea drinker judges tea.

But it takes long, patient processing to develop the color, fragrance, and flavor of tea from the sensitive green leaf after it has been picked.

When the tea plant sends out new shoots, it produces two tender young leaves and a small, unopened bud. These two leaves and bud are picked by hand. Usually, no older leaves are taken. Plucking, as it is called, is done mostly by women. In hot climates, the bushes may sprout and be ready for plucking every seven or eight days. In cooler areas it may take nearly twice as long. Flushing may slow down or even stop in colder weather.

The tea gardens are a festive sight during plucking. Bracelets gleam from slender wrists as the pluckers, wearing the vivid colors of the Orient, work their way through the dark green, waist-high tea bushes. With amazing speed, their quick fingers choose the leaves to be plucked, break them off with thumb and forefinger, and toss them into tall baskets tied to their backs or balanced on their heads.

An experienced plucker can pick as many as forty pounds of leaf in one day, enough to make nearly ten pounds of tea leaves. At the end of each day, the plucker's harvest is picked over for stalks and then weighed. Then the leaves begin their long journey to your teapot. The first step of that journey is the factory. Most large plantations have their own, whereas small estates send their harvest to centrally located factories. A summary of the process follows:

Withering The leaves are thinly spread to wither either naturally, where the climate is suitable, or by means of warm, dry air forced over the withering-racks. The object is to evaporate much of the tea leaf's water content so that the leaf becomes soft and pliable, like soft leather gloves. Green tea, however, is not given the withering treatment. Immediately after it is plucked it is put into a large steamer and heated. This method softens the leaves for rolling and keeps the juices from oxidizing. The leaves are then rolled and dried again and again until crisp. They remain green. Oolong tea, a compromise between black and green tea, has leaves that are only partly oxidized. They turn a greenish brown.

Rolling The softened leaf passes from the withering-racks to the rolling machinery. There it is twisted and rolled to separate the leaf cells and release the juices that flavor tea. The degree of the twist affects the rate of infusion. At this stage, the first important chemical change starts when the juices that remain on the leaf are exposed to the air and development of the essential oils begins.

Roll-Breaking From the roller tea leaves emerge as twisted lumps that are broken up by coarse mesh sieves, or roll-breakers. The fine leaf that falls through is taken to the fermenting room, while the coarse leaf is returned for further rolling.

Oxidation or Fermentation The oxidation that started in the rollers is completed in the fermenting room. Here the tea leaves are spread on cement or tiled floors (sometimes on glass or cement tables) in a cool, damp atmosphere. The leaves undergo a further chemical change through the absorption of oxygen, and turn a bright copper color, like a new penny. It is this process of oxidation that distinguishes the black teas, almost universally drunk in the United States today, from green teas.

Drying or Firing The purpose of this step is to arrest further oxidation, and to dry the leaf evenly and thoroughly without scorching it. The automatic tea drier consists of a large iron box, inside which the leaves, spread on trays, travel slowly from top to bottom while a continuous blast of hot dry air is forced into the box. Careful regulation of the temperature and of the speed at which the trays move is the main factor in successful firing.

Tea Has Many Grades as Well as Varieties

All told there are more than 3000 varieties of tea. Like wines, these take their names from the districts where they are grown.

Before the little leaves are ready to yield their flavorful brew to you, more processing experiences await them. As the leaves come from the drier, large and small, broken and unbroken leaves are mixed together. Now they must go through sieves, with graduated mesh, to sort them for distribution commercially. These sieves divide them into leaf and broken grades.

Black tea is graded by the size of its leaf. Leaf grades are made up of the larger leaves left after the broken grades have been sifted out. In brewing, flavor and color come out of leaf grades more slowly than out of broken grades. Leaf grades are popular in Continental Europe and South American countries. They are known as Orange Pekoe, Pekoe, and Pekoe Souchong.

Broken grades that are made up of smaller and broken leaves represent roughly 80 percent of the total crop. These make a darker, stronger tea. They are the choice in all countries except those mentioned above. These grades are essential for use in teabags, since they yield their color and flavor faster than the leaf grades, and are very popular in this country. The broken grades are divided into Broken Orange Pekoe, Broken Pekoe, Broken Pekoe Souchong, Fannings, and Fines (sometimes called Dust).

Americans frequently believe they are getting a certain quality of tea when they buy Orange Pekoe (pronounced peck-o, not peek-o). Because of the white appearance of the leaves, the Chinese referred to it as *pekoe*, which in their language means "white hair." The Chinese sometimes scented these leaves with orange blossoms; hence our term, "Orange Pekoe."

Today Orange Pekoe simply represents size; when you buy Orange Pekoe you are getting a size of tea leaf just as you buy a size of shoe or glove. Orange pekoe has nothing to do with the type, flavor, or quality of the tea. There may be a Darjeeling Orange Pekoe, Assam Orange Pekoe, and so on, through all the various black teas from the finest to the coarser qualities. The Pekoe, Souchong, Fannings, and Fines designations are used to indicate size only of black teas. A brief description of the grades follows:

Orange Pekoe   Long, thin, wiry leaf, that sometimes contains yellow tip or bud leaf. The liquors are light or pale in color.

Pekoe   The leaves of this grade are shorter and not so wiry as Orange Pekoe, but the liquors generally have more color.

Souchong   A bold and round leaf, with pale liquors.

Broken Orange Pekoe   Much smaller than any of the leaf grades, usually contains yellow tip. The liquors have good color and strength in the cup and are the mainstay of a blend.

Broken Pekoe Souchong   A little larger or bolder than Broken Pekoe and consequently lighter in the cup. Also used as a filler.

Fannings   Much smaller than Broken Orange Pekoe. Its main virtues are quick brewing with good color in the cup.

Fines   This is the name for the smallest grade produced. Very useful for a quick-brewing, strong cup of tea; used only in blends of similar-sized leaf, generally for catering purposes.

Green teas are quality-graded by a system that takes into account both the age and style of the leaf. Some of the better green grades from China will be labeled Gunpowder, Young Hyson, or Imperial. Japanese teas come under a different system, in which the highest grade is called Extra Choicest. Still another set of grade names is used for Indian greens, with the best called Fine Young Hyson. Oolong tea is classifed by yet another grading system. Formosa Oolong is graded strictly for quality, on an eighteen-point scale that runs from standard to choice.

How Tea is Sold and How U.S. Government Tea Standards are Established

Just as tobacco is sold at auction in the United States, so is tea auctioned. Tea must be examined and sampled if it is to be bought wisely, and auctions give buyers this opportunity.

The world's great auction centers are Calcutta and Cochin in India, Colombo in Sri Lanka, Jakarta in Indonesia, Mombasa in East Africa, and London. The price of that cup of tea you are drinking probably was determined at an auction in one of those cities. The United States receives its tea either direct from the countries where it was grown or through London.

Before the auction the tea chests are arranged

Teatime

side by side in long rows in the warehouse. A hole is bored in each chest and a sample of the tea it contains taken out. These samples are then sent to the leading tea buyers. If a buyer likes the sample he or she bids on it. Sometimes as many as 50,000 chests, or 5,000,000 pounds, of tea are sold in one day at these auctions.

Having made the highest bid and bought the tea, the buyer either ships it to fill an order, or sends samples to importers throughout the world. Most of the American importers or the packers who buy this tea direct are located in the major tea-buying centers of New York, Boston, Philadelphia, Chicago, New Orleans, Los Angeles, San Francisco, and Seattle.

American importers test samples of tea and order those they wish to buy. Then the tea starts its sea voyage to the United States, which usually takes seven weeks from Calcutta. As the aluminum foil-lined tea chests arrive in the principal U.S. ports of entry for tea, they are placed in bonded warehouses. By provisions set forth in the Tea Act of 1897, the tea cannot be moved from these warehouses until it is either approved or disapproved for entry by the U.S. Board of Tea Experts, which determines the high standards for tea in this country.

This Board—which operates under the Food and Drug Administration, but is paid for by the tea industry—is an outstanding example of government and business cooperation. Its members are six men chosen from the tea trade and one from the government. The U.S. Board of Tea Experts meets once each year, usually in February or March. The purpose of this meeting, held in the office of the government member in New York, is to set up minimum standards for the tea you will drink during the following year.

These standards go into effect on May 1 of each year.

Board members seat themselves at a round table and brew the tea to be judged for exactly five minutes in the little white cups that ring the table. Each man watches the leaves as they unfold. He sniffs the aroma. He takes some of the wet leaves from each cup with a spoon. He judges the color and aroma of the leaves. Then he checks the liquid itself for color and aroma. The leaves must be fresh and pure.

Perhaps one hundred samples of tea are submitted to the Board and judged during its annual meeting. The Board members decide upon a minimum standard for the year for each of the principal varieties of tea. Teas that do not meet this standard will not be admitted to the United States. Most of the 200 million pounds of tea imported into the country each year, though, is of higher grade than standard.

Should an importer object to the rejection of his tea by the U.S. Board of Tea Experts, he may take his case to the Board of Appeals. This Board, made up of three members, will call in three different tea tasters from the trade to judge the rejected tea. The decision of this Board is final. If it rejects the tea the shipment will not be permitted to enter. Because of this democratic system, no other country in the world enjoys higher quality tea than the United States.

America Blends and Packages Its Tea

After your tea, passed by the Board of Tea Experts, arrives in the United States, it must go through more important processes before it reaches you. Almost all our tea has been blended before it reaches the retailer. Tea companies blend their own distinctive brands that you can recognize by their packages.

Tea in its natural state is a variable product. The quality and amount from each bush may vary not only from season to season, but even from week to week. By blending a number of varieties of teas—sometimes as many as twenty or more—a company can protect the flavor of its brand from any great changes in the quality of one variety. In this way it can maintain a constant quality throughout the year. These blends are usually a carefully guarded secret.

It is the companies' tea tasters who determine how the different teas should be blended. Tea tasting is an art. An expert tea taster can identify between 1500 and 1600 different teas. In many cases the taster can take a few dried tea leaves and tell you where they were grown, what variety of tea they are, at what season of the year they were picked, and how they were processed. Such an expert can also tell you how much the tea should cost and how it should be blended with other teas.

The bulk blending is done in a large drum into which the contents of the chests are tipped. The inside of the blending drum is so designed that when the drum is rotated the leaves are thoroughly mixed. As the tea comes out of the drum, it is conveyed to automatic weighing and packing machines. When packaging loose tea, the blend is tipped in at the top, weighed into quarter pounds or half pounds as desired, and comes out as a complete, labeled package.

A battery of packing machines in action is something to see and hear—the clatter of the many intricate cams and levers that start by clutching a piece of cardboard and turning it into a package. It is filled with tea, sealed and labeled, and finally put on a conveyor belt all in a matter of seconds. Teabags also are packed in a wholly mechanical operation. One machine carefully weighs out the amount of tea and places it in each bag. Then it seals the bags, attaches strings and tags, and places them in cartons or tins.

Instant teas, a modern development in the tea industry, are prepared using a highly concentrated brew of tea from which the water is removed by a drying process. The soluble powder is measured automatically into glass jars and labeled. Even newer on the market are the iced tea mixes. Packaged in jars, envelopes, or canisters, the mixes are a combination of instant tea, flavorings, and sugar; low-calorie versions are also available. And you can buy liquid iced tea in flip-top cans, too.

At last the tea—loose, in individual bags, in powder form, or in cans—is ready for your grocer. It may go directly to him from the packer or through the hands of wholesalers or jobbers. By the time it reaches your grocer's shelf, however, all the varied steps in processing your tea have been completed. Many months have passed since the little leaves were picked on a hillside in far away India, Ceylon, Indonesia, or Africa. The long journey down great mountains and rivers, through distant foreign cities and over strange oceans to your tea cup, is ended. Here are some teas you're likely to find in your tea shopping:

Assam Rich black tea from Assam in northern India; its brew has heavy reddish color. Highly regarded by connoisseurs of India teas. This tea can be enjoyed at any time of the day, but especially in the morning, and is best served with milk.

Ceylon Breakfast A blend of Ceylon teas; a bit milder than English Breakfast or Irish Breakfast. For those that like a delicately flavored tea at any time of the day. Serve with lemon; it is especially good iced.

Darjeeling Full-bodied black tea harvested only a few months each year high in the foothills of the Himalayas, near Darjeeling, India. A rare and costly tea, famous for its muscatel flavor. Appropriate in the early afternoon, or after a curry dish. Can be served hot with milk or lemon.

Earl Grey aromatic black teas (usually China with Darjeeling), delicately scented. A famous English blend, originally from a recipe given in 1830 by a mandarin of China to an envoy sent out by Earl Grey, prime minister of Britain. An exceptional fragrance, and the epicure's choice among scented teas. A favorite afternoon tea, but enjoyed throughout the world at all times of the day. Sipped in the cool of the night by some, and with sweetmeats by others. Can be enjoyed with or without milk, according to preference.

English Breakfast A typical English blend of India and Ceylon black teas. A full-bodied, robust, richly colored brew that is a favorite for morning, but ideal at any time of the day. Serve hot with milk or lemon, or iced.

Gunpowder   Green tea with a tightly curled leaf. One of the finest green teas, with a pungent flavor. Best served after a Chinese meal, or after dinner on a hot evening, it is believed to have the lowest caffeine content of all teas.

Irish Breakfast   A robust blend, especially favored in Ireland. A blend of India or Ceylon black teas, with a pungent, aromatic brew. Particularly enjoyable on a cold, wet afternoon, with milk, or when taken in the morning with a hearty breakfast.

Jasmine Tea   Jasmine petals added to Oolong tea produce a pale, but heady brew with a distinctive flowery, exotic aroma. Perfect in the afternoon, after dinner, or in the late evening, sipped slowly with lemon, if desired, but not milk.

Keemum   A black tea that can be traced back to the ancient courts of Imperial China. Mellow with a superb bouquet; described as the burgundy of teas. Can be enjoyed with or after an Oriental meal, particularly in the afternoons and evenings, with or without milk. It is delicious iced.

Lapsang Souchong   One of the finest teas. From the Lapsang district, it is a large-leaf China tea with a distinctive smoky flavor. Appropriate after dinner, or on a hot afternoon or evening. Serve it hot without milk, or iced with lemon.

Russian Caravan A blend of fine quality China and Taiwan Oolong teas, which gives a superb fragrant brew that was so liked by the aristocracy of Russia that it was brought across Asia to Russia by camel caravan. For afternoons and evenings, with or without milk. Makes delicious iced tea.

Formosa Oolong A large distinctive leaf, of unique character and fragrance; the liquor can best be likened to ripe peaches. Best served mid-morning, afternoon, or in the evening after a good meal, without anything added to spoil the pure delight it gives. A fabulous tea.

Some of these teas are named after the district in which they grow; Assam and Darjeeling, for example. Others are named after people: Queen Mary, Prince of Wales, Earl Grey, and so forth. The Russian Caravan tea is named in honor of the route to its trade. Some are named after the flavor which has been added to the tea, such as jasmine. And still others are named after their type, the size of their leaf, a combination of type and size, or after their use. Examples of the latter are the breakfast teas—English, Irish, and Ceylon—those robust, full-bodied blends that are perfect morning beverages.

Why People Should Drink Tea

Tea is a light beverage and easily digested. It's refreshing, relaxing, reviving, and sets a time to communicate, even with oneself. In the world of stress, strain, and overkill, there is a need to unwind, and tea can provide the basis to release those nervous tensions. It is pleasant, harmless, and inexpensive. So, why not revive the custom and connoisseurship of yesterday? We could all do with a few more civilized influences.

Tea is regarded as a highly adaptable beverage. It can be made in different strengths; it can be used for a variety of occasions; and, of major significance, it is considered both stimulating and relaxing.

Here, as elsewhere, changing tides and conditions create changing habits. For many changers, regardless of the reasons they switched, tea drinking has become an integral part of daily living. Defectors from coffee do become confirmed tea drinkers for whom tea becomes the preferred mealtime beverage. It is forecast that by the early 1990's, America will consume as much tea as Great Britain.

Properly made tea helps you feel relaxed and refreshed. It gives a gentle lift, a feeling of well-being, due primarily to the caffeine and tannins in tea. Caffeine, the stimulant, is found in many things we eat or drink—chocolate, cocoa, coffee, and the cola beverages. The average cup of tea, when made according to package directions, contains about three-quarters grain of caffeine. On a comparative basis, the average cup of coffee contains about $1\frac{1}{2}$ grains of caffeine.

A pound of loose tea, using one teaspoon per cup, will make about 200 cups of tea, whereas a pound of coffee makes about fifty cups. If you use teabags, the same proportion holds true: a pound of tea is used to fill 200 teabags, enough for 200 cups. In the case of instant tea, one-half cup of powder in four quarts of water makes about twenty servings.

Comparing the number of cups of tea and the cost of tea per pound, you will find that next to water, tea is the least expensive beverage in the world, costing about two cents a serving. But, more than that, the pleasure and enjoyment one gets from properly made tea explain why tea is the most popular drink in the world:

> A nice cup of tea in the morning,
> For it starts the day you see—
> At half-past eleven, my ideal of Heaven,

Is a nice cup of tea.
I like a nice cup of tea with my dinner,
And a nice cup of tea with my tea—
And when it's time for bed,
There's a lot to be said
For a nice cup of tea.

Thomas Sullivan "Had it in the Bag!"

Tea is oriental in origin, European in refinement, but American it its fullest exploitation.

It was the year 1904 that brought about the discovery of both teabags and iced tea.

Thomas Sullivan, an enterprising tea and coffee merchant in New York, sent a few samples of tea in little bags to his customers. Such samples usually were sent in small tins, but Sullivan decided it would be simpler and less expensive to put the tea in small bags. He ordered several hundred little silk, hand-sewn bags, filled them with tea, and sent them to his customers. To Sullivan's great surprise, orders began to pour in for tea packed in the silk bags. His customers had discovered that by pouring boiling water over the bags, they could make tea with less effort.

Like iced tea, the teabag has become as symbolic of America as corn on the cob. It has become so popular in the United States that more than one-half of all the tea drunk here today is made with teabags. Now they are made of a special filter paper, and the manufacture of teabags has become a fine art and sizeable industry in itself.

How to Make the Perfect Cup of Tea

Yes, it's the boiling and brewing that are the important factors to the perfect cup. With so many world-famous blends available today, let me give you the correct tea "Drill":

1. Rinse out the kettle of its contents and start with fresh, cold tap water.
2. The trick is to bring the water to its *first* rolling boil. NEVER OVERBOIL! Overboiling takes the oxygen out of the water, which in turn creates a flat beverage. Turn heat down.
3. Take the teapot to the kettle and rinse out the pot with the hot water from the kettle. Never take the kettle to the teapot, as you lose one degree of heat per second, and hot water for tea must be 212°.
4. Use one teabag or teaspoon of loose tea per cup. Leaves enter the warm pot and the infusion starts as the leaf starts to open up.
5. Pour hot water, gently, over the leaves. (Never bruise the leaves.)
6. Allow the tea to brew for a minimum three to five minutes, according to the blend of tea and how you like your tea.

It's in the brewing that you get the aroma, fragrance, and flavor. You can then serve the perfect cup of tea.

Looking for a Teapot

There is a great array of teapots—in porcelain, earthenware, glass, ceramic, and so on—ranging from the very simplest to the almost formal. A teapot may cost from five to 250 dollars (the latter in silver, copper, or hand-painted porcelain), and true tea drinkers like to have several around.

The English and the French continue to make the notable round shapes in high-fired floral decorated porcelain. The oriental style, on the other hand, in stoneware or other pottery, tends to a straighter, cylindrical shape or a flatter, round one. Oriental versions often have bamboo handles to protect hands from the heat of the boiling water. Some Oriental pots have lovely raised enamel decorations. Americans, too, are producing their own in hand-thrown pottery. Watch out, though, for the design of the spout and lip. Many look delightful, but pour incorrectly.

To keep the tea hot, the old-fashioned tea cozy is back. I call it "The Hat to the Teapot"—available in quilted cotton prints and in chrome-plated metal. My preference in teapots is porcelain or earthenware, as either retains the heat that much better, which is so important in making tea.

Other pointers to teapots. Make sure the lid has a hole in it, and doesn't fall off when you pour. Also, the best teapots do not heat up the handle. Many sterling and metal pots do, and I would think twice before buying them.

Ultimately, the spout is most important. If badly designed, the tea will pour unevenly. It should pour smoothly. The lip is a must to be inspected, so that it does not drip, as many do. And when buying a teapot, do handle it to see if it's well-balanced. Fill it with water to see how it pours. Check if it's easy to use when brewing.

Myself, I am a collector of teapots, which is a fun hobby. I have so many, some people think I am "potty."

Kettles

Kettles play a very important part in making a perfect cup of tea, and I would recommend that some thought be given before buying one. Some metals affect the water. The best kettles are made with a chromium-plated copper body; black-molded, plastic heat-insulated handle; and lid knob. The Rolls-Royce of kettles is the British *Swan Range*. Today, the company manufactures electric kettles, which operate by a vapor-control switch that switches off as soon as the kettle boils. A reset button is provided to switch on or to reboil. This kettle has a great future throughout the world and is available in America from Tea Ambassador Enterprises Ltd., P.O. Box 5268, Scottsdale, Arizona 85261.

Teacups

Teacups are strictly a matter of taste. Among the teacups are small one-cup versions, one of which is like that formerly sold in Oriental train stations to carry aboard. The top, which doubled as a cup, was returned at the end of the trip. Little square stands with a round opening in the top to hold the cup, so the traveler doesn't burn his or her hands, still are available. So are small tables (sometimes nests of them), on which to set the tea things.

Teacups without handles in the Oriental manner are made usually in the same patterns as the pots and are sold as matching sets.

The Elevensey Cup

With the popularity of mugs all over the world, I realize it is impossible to make a perfect cup of tea, as you cannot retain the heat during the brewing period. You would never leave the lid off the teapot. In retaining the heat, the leaves are able to yield the full aroma, fragrance, and flavor. So, I donned my pith helmet—I should tell you, I keep most of my tea secrets and information under my hat—and behold, I remember China, where tea was first discovered by the Emperor Shen Nung. There tea became established as a social art. The porcelain teacups themselves were works of art, and *Cheinware* cups with lids were used for tea tastings by connoisseurs. (Professional tea tasters still use lidded bone china cups for this reason.)

The *Elevensey Cup* was designed by me in honor of the 11:00 A.M. tea break in Great Britain. Its design allows you to obtain maximum aroma, flavor, and fragrance, and to produce the perfect "cuppa" tea. It also keeps your tea hot. (Please note, no more dunking and no more brown water.) The *Elevensey Cup*, in fact, is ideal for people on the go, and a must for tea drinkers during working hours. It's great for use in the home if you want to make a quick cup of tea without using a large teapot. It's perfect after skiing, tennis, hunting, or any sport that leaves you in need of a quick pick-me-up.

INSTRUCTIONS: Here's how to enjoy a perfect "cuppa" with me!

1. Rinse out your kettle and start with fresh cold water.
2. Bring the water to its first rolling boil (again, never overboil—overboiled water will make flat tea, no matter how good the tea is).
3. Put a teabag into your *Elevensey Cup*.
4. Gently pour the water over the teabag.
5. Put the lid on the cup and allow the tea to steep from three to five minutes, according to taste.
6. Remove the lid and use it as a coaster for the cup. You can also put the used teabag on it.
7. If you are called away from your "cuppa," replace the lid on the cup to keep the tea hot.

The *Elevensey Cup* is available in sets of two, four, or six. For futher information, please write to: Tea Ambassador Enterprises Ltd., P.O. Box 5268, Scottsdale, Arizona 85261.

Infusers

Infusers are a perforated gadget for encasing the tea leaves. In this manner, you do not have to strain them out of the finished brew. There are various shapes to infusers, but the best is the ball shape. Most are on chains that hang over the side of the teapot. Especially useful for making a single cup is an infuser in the shape of a spoon, with a longer handle.

Tea Storage

Tea is delicate, and absorbs moisture and flavor. For this reason, airtight canisters should be used. The life and fragrance will continue indefinitely in this manner. What can cause tea to deteriorate if left open, particularly in the kitchen, are the odors from cooking that are picked up by the leaves.

Strong light or heat also can affect tea. So I would recommend you keep it in a cool area, always making sure the lid is snug, to keep it airtight. English tin "tea caddies" are available throughout the world and are perfect for protecting tea.

Drinking Your Tea

The connoisseur drinks his tea as is, to appreciate its full fragrance and flavor. I prefer one teaspoon of honey in my tea, as it's a lubricant for the throat and, in my opinion, tastes better than sugar. Also, choose your favorite preserves and use one teaspoon in your tea. It's most enjoyable. I did it—when my mother was not looking!

Should you use lemon and sugar, make sure you put the sugar in first, stir it, and then add the lemon. If you reverse this procedure, the chemical reaction of the lemon doesn't allow the sugar to dissolve quickly. And never use any form of cream. It affects the tannin and curdles. Milk only, please!

We British put our milk in the cup first (though I am told that Her Majesty Queen Elizabeth II puts it in after!). We first put milk into the cups because our bone china was so delicate, it would avoid breaking the cup. Today, we do it for another reason: should the tea be too strong, and you can tell before you fill the cup, the presence of milk dilutes the strength. Remember now, milk only and never any form of cream! The tannin in tea causes cream to curdle.

Tea for a Party? Here's the Answer—Fast and Foolproof!

I have a hot tip for making tea for a crowd—the easy way. You don't have to worry about last-minute boiling and brewing to produce a good "cuppa."

Just make it ahead of time in a concentrate. When the party is ready, the tea concentrate needs only the addition of boiling water for a perfect tea service. Here is my secret tea formula for a pleasant tea party without hassle for the hostess:

TEA FOR A PARTY: This amount will serve 25. Adjust proportions to the size of your party.

1. Have ready 2/3 measuring cup of loose tea.

Teatime

2. Bring one quart fresh cold water to a rolling boil.
3. Rinse out large teapot (at least a quart capacity) with boiling water, and add tea.
4. Pour quart of boiling water over tea, cover, and brew for five minutes.
5. Stir and strain into quart pitcher or teapot. Keep at room temperature.
6. The tea concentrate should be used *within four hours*. When the party's ready, pour two tablespoons of tea concentrate into each cup and fill with fresh boiling water.

NOTE: Tea concentrate is fine for iced tea, too. Use 2½ tablespoons per glass; add ice and cold water.

Other Important Hints for Preparing Tea

1. The best way to test good teas is to hold the leaves up to the light. The better teas have brighter leaves, but a tea that turns dark and dull when you brew it is poor quality.
2. Believe it or not, most people have a tendency to overboil water. In doing so they are taking the oxygen out of the water, which, in turn, creates a flat beverage no matter how good the tea may be.
3. It's just as bad if the water you use has not reached a rolling boil. Half the leaves will float to the top of the teapot and remain there during the brewing. To judge the heat of the water, take a tip from profes-

sionals in the tea business, who use a brewing technique they call "laying a carpet." When they spread the tea at the bottom of the cup or pot and pour over it water that has been sufficiently boiled, the tea leaves roll up through the water, distributing their flavor, and then settle again on the bottom.

4. Do not judge the strength of tea by color. Some teas brew light, others dark. Brew by the clock.

5. If you like weak tea, add a little hot water to your tea after the full brewing period. In Great Britain, they serve hot water in a jug for this purpose, and for filling the teapot should you wish a second cup. I am sure you have heard the expression, "And one for the pot."

6. Stir tea before pouring to make sure it's uniformly strong.

7. Use the teabag once. You take ninety-eight of the strength the first time you use it—the remaining two percent will give you nothing but slop! Instead, the used teabag can be used for enhancing the growth of roses; for treating minor burns, particularly during cooking; and for reducing puffiness under the eyes.

Iced Tea

Although more than 4000 years have passed since Emperor Shen Nung discovered tea, his experience had great bearing on a more recent discovery that took place in St. Louis, during the Louisiana Purchase Exposition in 1904. Before the Exposition, many changes toward modern living had taken place: courageous sailors found their way to China from Europe; Columbus discovered America; the world witnessed the birth of United States and its growth as a major power. For all those thousands of years, no one had even thought of drinking tea anyway but hot. It remained for America to give the world iced tea.

The story of the discovery of iced tea bears comparison with the Chinese and Indian versions of the discovery of tea. Richard Blechynden, a young Englishman, had come all the way from Calcutta, India, to represent teas from the Far East at the Exposition. With Blechynden came several handsome young Singhalese, as the people of Ceylon were called. Wearing brightly colored turbans and jackets, these young men served tea to the visitors at the Exposition. Their mission was, of course, to help popularize tea.

But the weather turned stifling hot. Day after day, the perspiring crowd hurried past the colorful Far East tea house where hot tea was being served to areas where iced drinks were available. In desperation, Blechynden began to experiment. He tried filling tall glasses with pieces of ice and pouring hot tea into them—if people wanted iced drinks, he would give it to them. It's what we call, in our country, using your "loaf" or your head.

The cool copper-colored liquid surrounding the ice in the glasses looked tempting to the parched fairgoers. Here was something new. They found the new drink so cooling and refreshing that they asked for more. By the time the Exposition closed, iced tea had already become a popular drink. Its popularity has continued to increase steadily each year. Today, it is America's national summertime drink. It is rather a shame that iced tea is not more popular throughout the world; I can only assume it is due to the lack of refrigeration elsewhere. I am confident that as this situation improves, it will enjoy the same popularity.

I make my iced tea the cold water method. In this country, it is called "sun tea." Most people are of the impression that the sun has some effect on the tea and creates its crystal clarity. Frankly, that's a lot of nonsense. What makes iced tea cloudy is hot water. The cold water method allows the leaves to steep naturally in the cold water, thus creating the crystal-clear effect. The difference, especially in the taste, is amazing.

There's no question, iced tea is not only refreshing, but surely the number one thirst-quenching beverage in the world. I enjoy adding orange and lemon slices with fresh mint; I would like to see the use of more orange in tea. It makes a delightful combination. Try it!

Four Good Reasons to Drink Iced Tea:

1. It's economical—costs less than four cents a glass, including sugar and lemon.
2. Its fresh, clean taste really quenches thirst, and leaves no sticky, sweet aftertaste to build up another thirst.
3. It won't add unwanted calories if you drink it plain. Even with a teaspoon of sugar and a squeeze of lemon, it contains only 20 calories.
4. Iced tea makes a perfect base for a party punch. The tea gives body to the punch without masking the

Teatime

flavors of the other ingredients. Try combining iced tea with your choice of fruit juices—orange, pineapple, cranberry, lemon, apricot, or a combination of any of these. Sweeten to taste.

Basic Directions for Iced Tea When preparing tea to be served iced, make it extra strong; use fifty percent more tea than usual to allow for melting ice. In other words, you use 4 teabags or 4 teaspoons of loose tea to make 4 cups of hot tea, but for 4 glasses of iced tea you need 6 teabags. Pour boiling water over teabags in a teapot or saucepan with cover. Let stand for 5 minutes. Strain. Pour into iced-filled glasses.

Iced Tea for a Crowd For beach picnics or outdoor barbecues, the simplest way to make a gallon of iced tea (enough for 20 servings) is to use instant tea powder. Allow ½ measuring cup instant tea to 4 quarts cold water. Stir to dissolve; add ice.

Iced Tea: The Cold Water Method A new no-work method using teabags and cold water produces crystal-clear iced tea guaranteed never to cloud. Just remember to start it at least 6 hours before you plan to serve. "Rosie Lee and the Fisherman's Daughter do all the work." "Rosie Lee and the Fisherman's Daughter?" That's tea and water. What else? Here's how I make it, without the sun:

1. Fill a quart pitcher or container with cold tap water.
2. Add 8–10 teabags.

3. Cover. Let stand at room temperature or in the refrigerator.

4. Then, after 6 hours or overnight, tea's ready, cool, and crystal clear. Just remove the teabags, squeezing them against the side of the container first. When ready to serve, pour into ice-filled glasses.

Iced Tea by the Pitcherful   For family service, use this easy 2-quart formula (enough for 10 servings). Bring 1 quart of freshly drawn cold water to a full rolling boil in a saucepan. Remove from heat and immediately add 15 teabags or ⅓ cup loose tea. Stir, cover, and let stand 5 minutes. Stir again and strain into a pitcher holding another quart of cold water. Keep at room temperature. When ready to serve, pour into ice-filled glasses.

Iced Tea Made with a Mix   With an envelope or jar of iced tea mix on hand you can have sweetened, flavored iced tea in an instant. Check package directions, as amounts to use may vary. In general, 1 envelope mixed with 2 cups (1 pint) water makes 3 servings. For a single glass, use 3 teaspoons mix; for a quart pitcher, ½ cup of mix.

Iced Tea: The Instant Way   For convenience and ease of preparation anytime, anyplace, nothing beats instant tea powder. It dissolves instantly in cold water and you can adjust the strength by varying the amount of powder you use. For a pitcherful use 2 rounded tablespoons of tea powder for each quart of cold water. Stir and add ice. For one glass of iced tea, use a rounded teaspoon of instant tea for each 6–8 ounces of cold water.

Why Not Blend Your Own Teas?

It's possible! I can assure you that it's not difficult and that one doesn't need to be an expert. Anyone can blend teas by simply adding a small amount of another kind to the blend generally used.

Many confirmed tea drinkers with trial and error can blend tea rather well. Tea drinking follows moods. Today, it may be Oolong. Tomorrow, your mood may be to add a little Darjeeling. Blending teas follows the same principle as blending wines: they are blended to suit one's palate.

I have an old Victorian tea-blending box, which has a compartment on each side of the box for two different blends of teas. And in the middle, between the compartments, is a glass bowl. By taking a little of both blends and mixing them in the bowl with any of my favorite spices, I have been rewarded in tasting many new delightful tea blends.

British Social Custom

The Beginnings of Informal Teatime

"It's 4:00! Time for tea!"

It was the Seventh Duke of Bedford's wife, Anna, who, during the eighteenth century, invented the English custom of afternoon tea—better known today as "set tea," which is a limited tea of finger sandwiches, tea biscuits, slices of cake, or pastry.

In those days, they ate prodigious breakfasts because lunch was not yet invented. Poor Anna! Around 4:00 P.M., she always had a sinking feeling, so she instructed her servants to bring her tea and cakes. This pastime soon got around the court circles and brought about "teatime," but for the rich only, as tea was extremely expensive.

Many years later, in 1785, George III allowed himself to be seen eating bread and butter and cake with his tea, and so the institution of tea, the meal, was born. It grew ever more elaborate, reaching its apotheosis in the Victorian "High Tea." High tea usually consisted of one or two small hot dishes, cold chicken, game, tongue, ham, salad, cakes of various kinds, and fruit tarts with cream or custard. (It's equivalent to an American light supper.) And in those days, the poor could not afford dinner, so they would take the remnants of their lunch and partake of it in the late afternoon, or early evening, with tea.

In Great Britain today, high tea is practically nonexistent except for parts of Northern England and Scotland. One can still enjoy in the countryside, however, the teatime ritual of strawberries, clotted cream and scones. It's a must, and most civilized!

Informal Tea Informal tea is always a gracious intimate gesture of hospitality. Its attendants are close friends, neighbors, or family; it has a "touch of class." Teatime is generally between three to five o'clock. In my country, 4:00 P.M. is the official hour.

The hostess serves from a small table in her living room, with chairs grouped around for her guests. The tea service is brought to the table on a large tray, or tea wagon, or tea trolley, as we call it in England. On the tray goes the teapot, sugar bowl, milk jug, plate of lemon or orange slices, cups, saucers, teaspoons, and napkins. The tea foods can be put on a table nearby. The food is usually light and easy to pick up with the fingers, though plates can be used. Buttered crumpets, finger sandwiches, scones, tea biscuits, pastries, or cake might be offered. The hostess pours the tea, offering her guests the choice of milk, lemon, or sugar, but the guests help themselves to the food. Tea is a time to share something good to eat in the comfortable presence of friends and family.

Second Version of Informal Tea (in England) Tea in an English home is laid on a dining room table on an embroidered tea cloth. There is a strict order of eating. First, savory, followed by thinly sliced sandwiches with cucumbers and tomatoes and watercress, usually from the kitchen garden. Then you have finely sliced buttered bread and homemade raspberry jam. After that, you have the choice, perhaps, of gingerbread squares, shortbread, slices of chocolate layer cake, or pieces of rich Dundee fruitcake. Children have milk as the grown-ups drink tea.

Formal Tea Formal tea is a most perfect way to meet and chat in a relaxing mood. It's a stand-up affair, in which refreshments are served in the dining room and living room, and one can eat and talk at the same time. The tea table is set with the tea service at one end and a companion service for punch or coffee at the other. The tea tray holds the teapot, a pot of hot water, the sugar bowl, milk jug, and a plate of lemon slices. Cups and saucers are placed generally to the left of the tray, with spoons lined up nearby. Stacks of plates, with napkins between each one, are lined up along the edge of the table. Fresh flowers and candles compose the traditional centerpiece. The platters of food range down the center, consisting of finger sandwiches, English tea biscuits, pastries, and cakes. The hostess does not serve the tea. She asks two of her friends to act as "pourers" while she supervises the replenishing of the foods, tea, and collection of empty cups.

Formal tea is an inexpensive way of entertaining. I have advised many charming young women throughout the world, particularly shy ones, to invite a "bloke" to tea. The results are surprising!

The Teas That Try One's Soul and Other Pretenders to the Throne

Oh, the trials and tribulations of trying to get a perfect cup of tea when dining out in the ex-colonies. It's almost impossible and sometimes amusing. To illustrate:

> I invited a dear friend of mine to lunch during a short stop in Monterey, California. The lunch was superb! I ordered Cornish Pasties, followed by tea. When the tea arrived, I complained to the waiter, "It tastes like benzine. You sure it's tea?" The waiter replied, "It must be, the coffee tastes like turpentine." I was determined then and there that it's about time we changed this uncivilized situation so the tea drinking public can enjoy a decent cup.

My message is a warning cry to all of us when dining out: "Protect your wicket! Beware of waitresses bearing warm water!"

How to Order Tea in Restaurants and Hotels

I am deeply concerned that the American tea drinker too often is not getting a fair deal in restaurants and hotels. As a result, few of us are inclined to order tea in public eating places.

We are being neglected, not by design but from ignorance. With some laudable exceptions, management in hotels and restaurants just do not know how tea should be brewed or served. Regrettably, they do not know the difference between brown water and a decent cup of "Rosie Lee."

Some tips for ordering hot tea in restaurants— both for the consumer who, despite the odds, would like to order a cup of tea when dining out, and for the restauranteur who has every hospitable and economic reason to serve it—follow:

1. Advise the management of whatever public eating house you are patronizing to be good enough to serve the tea in a pot, preferably a china or earthenware pot.

2. Suggest, not demand, that the water be boiling furiously when poured over the teabag. Never receive your tea with the teabag on the side. You lose one degree of heat per second. Consequently, the water is

not hot enough for the tea leaves to do their job properly.

3. And that the tea be brewed to the satisfaction of the customer, allow three to five minutes according to the tea drinker's choice.

4. Should the manager or the help demur, do not hesitate to point out that a pound of tea yields 200 cups, compared to only forty for a pound of coffee. Yet the price charged for a cup of either is the same!

5. And don't stop there. Remind the establishment that more satisfied customers mean more profits and that there is no more satisfied customer than a tea-drinking customer.

6. Although the most recommended teamanship calls for service in a pot rather than a cup, still one can make do with the latter if one is careful about the following: the teabag must be put in the cup first with boiling water poured over it, and then brought to the table; the teabag must never be used more than once. The rule for a second cup is a second teabag and, of course, a second serving of fresh boiling water.

7. Once the tea is brewed, remember what to do and what not to do with cream, milk, lemon and sugar. To wit: don't use the cream at all, use milk. If you use lemon rather than milk, put it in after the sugar; otherwise, the sugar won't dissolve.

8. Never underestimate the power of a teabag and its contents. The bag contains a blend of fine tea leaves. Give them a chance to open up gently and release their full fragrance and taste. Don't dunk the teabag up and down and don't rush it. It needs a minimum of three minutes' brewing to do its job.

In other words, with a little bit of care, we can have a cup that truly cheers.

The Tea That is Not a Tea— Herb Tea

It should be very clearly pointed out that herb teas are not teas. In the tea industry, herb teas are much scowled upon and the only connection between herbs and real teas is that both are infused in boiling water. There are, however, people who like them, so I am listing a few of them under the heading of "Tea Pharmacy":

Tea Pharmacy

Sage tea was known as a sore throat gargle.

Strawberry leaf tea cured babies with cankers.

Blackberry and raspberry teas were valued for bowel problems.

Camomile flower tea was named the "garden physician" for its milk and soothing tonic.

Borage tea was ideal for non drinkers and thinkers who wanted to be exhilarated.

Catnip, rich in vitamins A and C, was popular as a sleep inducer.

Pennyroyal tea broke up colds.

Tonia teas came from the roots of sassafras, gentian, sarsparilla, burdock, licorice and yellow dock.

Tan-Tea-Lizing Recipes

Hot Tea Recipes

BLACK TEA WITH GINGER ROOT

I recall a Hindu friend of mine making ginger tea to help cure a cold I had. The tea made me glow on its way down, but was most comforting and relieving. Brew your favorite black tea in the usual way, adding grated ginger root, honey, and lemon juice to taste.

TEA AND HONEY

Brew your favorite black tea as you usually do and add honey to taste. A must for people who sing or chat a lot!

CINNAMON TEA

Brew your black tea the regular way and include a stick of cinnamon in the brewing.

MINT TEA

1 tablespoon whole cloves
1 cup loose tea leaves
½ cup dried mint flakes
2 tablespoons dried diced orange peel

Wrap cloves in a piece of ripped cheesecloth or old sheeting. Pound with mallet until finely crumbled. In mixing bowl, stir together crumbled cloves, tea, mint flakes, and orange peel. Store in container with tight-fitting lid. Makes about 1½ cups. To brew, use 1 rounded teaspoonful of mint tea mixture for each teacup.

HOT SHOT TEA

4 tablespoons instant tea
2 quarts boiling water
½ cup honey
½ cup lemon juice
¼ teaspoon Tabasco
Lemon slices
Cinnamon sticks

Put instant tea into pitcher; add boiling water and stir to dissolve. Add honey, lemon juice, and Tabasco. Stir well to blend. Serve hot with a slice of lemon and cinnamon stick in each mug. Makes 12 servings.

Teatime

HONEY CUP

⅔ cup honey
2 egg yolks, beaten
2 cups hot strong tea*
Juice of 1 lemon

Mix honey well with the egg yolks. Add the hot tea slowly, stirring all the while. Stir in lemon juice and serve at once in tumblers.

*To make tea, bring 2 cups of freshly drawn cold water to a full, rolling boil. Pour over 2 teaspoons loose tea or 2 teabags. Let stand 5 minutes. Strain. Makes about 2¾ cups for 3 servings.

HONEYED SPICED TEA

4 teabags
4 cups boiling water
2 cups cider
1 3-inch cinnamon stick
6 cinnamon sticks
¼ teaspoon mace
½ teaspoon allspice
3 tablespoons honey
6 spiced crabapples, drained

Pour boiling water over tea. Cover and let steep 5 minutes. Remove teabags. Meanwhile, heat cider with spices and honey; boil 1 minute. Mix with hot tea. Serve in mugs with a crabapple in each. If desired, use long cinnamon sticks as muddlers. Makes about 6 servings.

THE COCKNEY CARDAMON

2 cups boiling water
1 teaspoon fennel
1 teaspoon cardamon seeds, crushed
2 tablespoons instant tea mix
1 tablespoon sugar
¼ teaspoon cinnamon

In small saucepan, combine water, fennel, and cardamon seeds. Boil for 2 minutes. Remove from heat; stir in instant tea mix, sugar, and cinnamon. Strain. Makes about 4 5-ounce servings.

LADY BLINKALOT'S CRANBERRY APPLE TEA

2 cups cranberry juice
2 cups apple juice
3 tablespoons instant tea mix
2 sticks cinnamon
8 whole cloves

In large saucepan, combine cranberry juice, apple juice, instant tea mix, cinnamon sticks, and cloves. Bring to boil; reduce heat and simmer 5 to 10 minutes. Strain. May be served hot or cold. Makes 8 4-ounce servings.

THE MERMAID PINEAPPLE TEA

1 18-ounce can pineapple juice
1 cup water
¼ cup instant tea mix
1 tablespoon sugar
Cinnamon sticks

Teatime

In large saucepan, combine pineapple juice, water, instant tea mix, and sugar. Cover and allow to simmer for 5 minutes. Serve hot and use cinnamon stick for muddler. Makes 4 6-ounce servings.

HER MAJESTY'S FLAVORED TEA

¼ cup mint jelly or marmalade
2½ cups water

5 teaspoons instant tea mix

In small saucepan, combine mint jelly or marmalade and water. Heat, stirring constantly, until jelly melts and mixture is hot. Stir in instant tea mix; let steep for 1 minute. Serve hot. Makes 4 5-ounce servings.

NOTE: Flavored tea may also be served individually by combining instant tea with boiling water, pouring it into a cup, and stirring in 2 to 3 teaspoons jelly.

CAPTAIN HOOK'S TEA GROG

8 teaspoons instant tea mix
¼ cup sugar

2 teaspoons orange juice
1 teaspoon cinnamon
¼ teaspoon cloves

In small bowl, combine instant tea mix, sugar, orange juice, cinnamon, and cloves; blend well. Place 2 measuring teaspoons grog base into cup or mug. Add boiling water and stir. Makes 4 6-ounce servings.

Iced Tea Recipes

THE LIMBO DIET DELIGHT

2 cups water
1½ cups pineapple juice
1 teaspoon rum extract
2 tablespoons low-calorie iced tea mix

In 1½-quart pitcher, combine water, pineapple juice, low-cal iced tea mix, and rum extract. Mix well. Serve over ice. Makes 4 7-ounce servings.

ROSEY LEE DIET FLOAT

¼ cup water
1 tablespoon low-calorie iced tea mix
1 scoop lemon sherbet
¾ cup black cherry-flavored low-calorie carbonated beverage

In tall glass, combine water and low-cal iced tea mix. Mix well. Stir in black cherry low-calorie soda. When foam disappears, top with a scoop of sherbet. Makes 1 serving.

AUBREY'S STRAWBERRY ICED TEA

1 10-ounce package frozen strawberries, thawed
1 6-ounce can frozen lemonade concentrate, thawed
½ cup sugar
½ cup instant iced tea mix
6 cups cold water

Teatime

In blender, combine strawberries, lemonade concentrate, sugar, and instant tea mix. Mix at high speed until smooth. Pour into serving pitcher; stir in cold water. Serve over ice with lemon slice, if desired. Makes twelve 4-ounce servings.

THE BOMBAY ICED-TEA SHAKE

2 cups cold water
2 scoops vanilla ice cream
  (½ cup each), softened
2 tablespoons instant
  tea mix
2 tablespoons sugar

In blender, combine water, ice cream, instant tea mix, and sugar. Blend at high speed for 10 seconds or until foamy and well mixed. Serve at once. Makes 3 servings.

THE HAYMAKER TEA NOG

1 egg, separated
3 tablespoons sugar
1½ cups milk
2 tablespoons instant tea
  mix

In small bowl, beat egg white until stiff but not dry. Beat in sugar gradually until stiff, glossy peaks form. In container of blender, combine milk, egg yolk, and instant tea mix; blend at high speed for 10 seconds. Gradually fold instant tea mixture into egg white. Pour into glasses. Makes 4 5-ounce servings.

ALMOND DELIGHT

4 cups water
6 tablespoons instant iced tea mix
6 tablespoons honey
½ cup orange juice
1½ teaspoons almond extract
2 cups ginger ale

In 2½ quart pitcher, combine water, instant iced tea mix, honey, orange juice, and almond extract. Stir until dissolved. Blend in ginger ale. Makes 12 4-ounce servings.

HENRY VIII LO-CAL SPECIAL

1 cup low-cal cranberry juice cocktail
1 tablespoon instant low-cal iced tea mix
2 12-ounce cans artificially sweetened citrus-flavored carbonated beverage

In 1 quart pitcher, combine cranberry juice and instant low-cal iced tea mix. Stir until dissolved. Slowly pour in citrus low-calorie soda and stir gently. Serve with ice cubes. Makes 4 8-ounce servings.

OPEN HOUSE PUNCH

2 quarts iced tea
2 cans frozen lemonade
2 cans frozen limeade
2 cups cranberry juice
2 28-ounce bottles ginger ale

Pour iced tea into a punch bowl. Stir in lemonade, limeade, cranberry juice. Add ginger ale and ice just before serving. Makes about 5 quarts or 40 punch-cup servings.

DARJEELING DEVIL

2 quarts Darjeeling
   iced tea
3 oranges
2 limes
2 cups sugar
10 whole cloves

Use two quarts iced tea. In separate bowl, squeeze oranges and limes, and save the rinds. Use pot, add two quarts of water, to sugar, cloves, and rinds. Boil 5 minutes. Remove from heat. Add orange and lime juice. Strain into iced tea. Cool to room temperature, and serve over ice. Makes about 20 servings.

NECTAR PUNCH

2 cups hot water
⅔ cup sugar
6 measuring tablespoons
   instant tea mix
1 teaspoon nutmeg
4 cups apricot nectar
3 cups cold water
½ cup lemon juice
1 quart raspberry
   flavored carbonated
   beverage

In 3-quart container, combine hot water, sugar, instant tea mix, and nutmeg. Stir until sugar and tea are dissolved. Add apricot nectar, cold water, and lemon juice. Chill in refrigerator until ready to serve. Pour into punch bowl; gradually stir in raspberry soda. Garnish punch cups with assorted chunks of fruit on skewers, if desired. Makes about 28 4-ounce servings.

LOGANBERRY (OR CRANBERRY) PUNCH

2 teaspoons or 2 teabags black tea
½ cup boiling water
1 cup loganberry or cranberry juice

1 small bunch fresh mint
½ cup sugar
Pinch of salt
1 pint ginger ale
Juice of 2 lemons

Brew tea for 3 minutes. Add sugar and salt and let cool. Add fruit juices and ginger ale. Pour over cracked ice and garnish with the fresh mint.

CAREFREE FRUIT PUNCH (WHIPPED TEA)

1 quart water
½ cup loose tea or 12 teabags
1 quart cold water
2 6-ounce cans frozen concentrated lemonade
2 6-ounce cans frozen limeade

2 cups cranberry juice cocktail
2 28-ounce bottles ginger ale
Orange and lemon slices

Bring one quart water to first boil. Pour gently over tea. Cover and brew. Stir and strain into punch bowl containing one quart cold water. Stir in concentrates and cranberry juice. Place block of ice or ice cubes in punch. Add ginger ale, orange and lemon slices. Spice to taste.

Spirited Teas

Tea, over the centuries, has been one of the most popular ingredients to mix with alcohol and spirits. It has been popularized in hot toddies, punches, brandied spiced tea, and so forth. I believe that in the next few years you will see many distillers produce liquors that are as suitable for teas as the ones available for coffee.

Queen Anne was said to have consoled herself for her ill health and dull husband by sipping "cold tea" (brandy in a cup). Here's a favorite of Queen Anne, who obviously liked her teas spirited:

> Make a quart of very excellently brewed tea. Pour it out and set it over the fire, and beat therein the yolks of four eggs, and a pint of white wine, a grated nutmeg, and sugar to taste. Stir over fire till very hot. Drink in china dishes. (Signed "Queen Anne," c. 1708.)

GEORGE IV RUM DRINK (c. 1825)

Peel of two oranges
Peel of twelve lemons
2 quarts rum
2 quarts cold spring water
1 pound loaf sugar
1 pint strong tea
¼ pint maraschino cordial
1 pint lemon juice
1 pint Madeira
1 grated nutmeg
1 pint boiling milk

Infuse the peels of the oranges and lemons in the rum for 12 hours; add to water, loaf sugar, tea, maraschino, lemon juice, Madeira, and nutmeg. Mix all ingredients together; stir in boiling milk last. Let stand for 6 hours, then strain through a jelly bag until quite clear and bottle for use.

ROYAL PUNCH

2 cups hot black tea
1 cup Jamaica rum
1 cup brandy
Sugar to taste
1 wine glass (8 ounces) white Curaçao
Juice of 2 lemons

Mix all ingredients and drink as hot as possible.

TEA DE MENTHE

3 bags mint tea
4½ cups boiling water
6 mint sprigs
¾ cup green creme de menthe
6 mint candy canes

Steep tea bags in boiling water for 5 minutes. Remove bags and stir liqueur into tea. Serve in mugs; garnish with mint sprig and candy cane. Makes 6 servings.

MANDARINE NAPOLÉON TANGERINE TEA

Mandarine Napoléon Liqueur is an ingratiating blend of Andalusian tangerines and aged cognac.

3 bags orange-spice tea
4½ cups boiling water
18 cloves
¾ cup Mandarine Napoléon Liqueur
6 lemon wedges

Steep tea bags in boiling water for 5 minutes. Remove bags and stir liqueur into tea. Serve in mugs; garnish with lemon wedge pierced with 3 cloves. Makes 6 servings.

SPARKLING TEA PUNCH

1 quart cold water
⅓ cup loose tea or 15 teabags
¼ cup rum
¼ cup brandy
Juice of 2 lemons
1 28-ounce bottle club soda, chilled
1 fifth Sparkling Burgundy, chilled
1 cup simple syrup*

Bring water to a full rolling boil in a saucepan. Remove from heat. Immediately add all the tea at one time. Brew 5 minutes. Stir and strain. Cool at room temperature. Combine rum, brandy, and lemon juice. Blend in tea concentrate. Chill. When ready to serve, pour into punch bowl. Add club soda and Sparkling Burgundy. Sweeten to taste with simple syrup. Makes about 25 servings.

*To make simple syrup, boil 1 cup water and 1 cup sugar for 5 minutes. Cool.

TEA SARONNO (TEA WITH LOVE)

My civilized answer to Irish coffee! It creates more than a "giggle"! Di Saronno is the original amaretto, dating back to 1525. It was invented by an attractive young widow who prepared this drink by using some almonds of apricot steeped in aquavit (a fusion of alcohol). The mixture resulted in a sweet, pleasing almond of apricot liqueur. Today it's known as Amaretto di Saronno and is extremely popular in this country. It is indeed a romantic-tasting liqueur!

In northern India, for many centuries, ground almonds were added to tea, giving relief to fatigue, anxiety, and tension, thus helping one to relax.

¾ cup (6 ounces) hot tea
1 8-ounce stemmed glass
Whipped cream
1½ ounce Amaretto di Saronno

Place a spoon into the stemmed glass to prevent breakage. Pour the freshly brewed tea into the glass. Remove spoon. Add the Amaretto. Do not stir. Top with lightly whipped cream. Sip through cream. Makes one serving. Ideal after dining, skiing parties, etc.

LORD HICCUPS TEA TODDY

2 tablespoons corn syrup
2 tablespoons lemon juice
1 cup tea
1 dash bitters
2 ounces vodka

Stir well in heatproof glass, fill with boiling hot tea, and decorate with spiral of lemon peel. Hope it's cured you!

RUM TEA PUNCH

1 cup brandy or rum
1 tablespoon sugar
1 cup tea
Cinnamon and nutmeg to taste
Milk
Juice of 1 lemon
Shaved ice

Brew tea in the usual way. Combine first four ingredients. Fill container half full of shaved ice and shake well. Strain. Add enough milk to fill the container. Dust with nutmeg and cinnamon as desired. Serve with a straw.

THE PERFORMER'S PUNCH

3 quarts cider
8 cups rum
8 cloves
8 cups Amaretto di Saronno or Mandarine Napoléon Liqueur
4 tablespoons sugar
1 lemon
1 orange
1 teaspoon ground cinnamon
1 teaspoon ground ginger
Rind from the fruit in thin strips

Peel the rind from the fruit in thin strips and chop finely. Slice fruit. Put ½ pint cider in a small saucepan. Add sugar and spices. Cover and simmer for 30 minutes. Pour the rest of the cider into a large saucepan. Add the strained fruit and spiced liquid. Heat slowly to a comfortable drinking temperature. Add the rum and Amaretto. Stir and heat once more. (Never overheat any alcohol mixture, otherwise its power will disappear.) Taste. Add more sugar if needed. Serves 10 to 12.

OLD MEDFORD PUNCH

1 quart Medford rum
1 cup claret
1 cup brandy or
   Mandarine Napoléon
   Liqueur

Sugar to taste
1 cup black tea
2 quarts champagne
3 sliced oranges
1 sliced pineapple

Mix the rum, claret, brandy, and tea. Sweeten to taste. Add the sliced fruit. Let stand for 24 hours. Chill. Add champagne and serve.

"LOVERLY" TEA PUNCH

3 12-ounce cans iced tea
   with lemon and sugar
1 8-ounce cup Amaretto
   di Saronno or
   Mandarine Napoléon
   Liqueur
1 6-ounce can frozen
   pineapple or orange
   juice concentrate,
   thawed, and undiluted

¼ cup lime or lemon juice
1 12-ounce bottle club
   soda or ginger ale
Ice cubes
Mint sprigs

In a 2-quart or larger pitcher, combine iced tea, Amaretto, pineapple juice, and lime or lemon juice. Chill thoroughly. When ready to serve, stir in club soda or ginger ale and add ice cubes. Pour into ice-filled glasses and garnish with mint sprigs, if desired. Makes about 2 quarts.

MAY WINE PUNCH

⅕ bottle (4/5 quart) May Wine
1 cup water
¼ cup Grand Marnier
2 tablespoons lemon-flavored instant tea mix
2 tablespoons confectioners sugar
1 12-ounce bottle ginger ale
Strawberries

In 2-quart pitcher, combine May Wine, water, Grand Marnier, tea mix, and confectioners sugar. Mix well. Stir in ginger ale. Serve over ice with a strawberry in each glass. Makes 8 5-ounce servings.

BLAZING JOHN PEEL

3 cups strong tea
6 tablespoons corn syrup
6 tablespoons orange juice
2 sticks cinnamon, broken
8 cloves
1 spiral orange peel
1 spiral lemon peel
1 cup dry gin or vodka

Divide tea among 3 cups. Place remaining ingredients in saucepan or blazing tin of chafing dish. Heat well, simmer a few minutes, ignite, and ladle into tea cups.

THE HYDE PARK GIGGLE

2 quarts (8 cups) water
4 1.7-ounce packages (1 cup) iced tea mix
4 teaspoons whole cloves
4 cinnamon sticks
4 teaspoons whole allspice
1 cup apple brandy or apple jack

Teatime

In 3-quart saucepan, combine water, iced tea mix, cloves, allspice, and cinnamon sticks; bring to boil. Lower heat and simmer 5 minutes. Strain into heat-proof punch bowl. Stir in apple brandy. Garnish with apple slices, if desired. Makes about 20 4-ounce servings.

ROYAL FUSILIERS TEA PUNCH

- 3 cups water
- ½ cup instant iced-tea mix
- 1 bottle (4/5 quart) bourbon
- 1 bottle (4/5 quart) claret
- 2 cups orange juice
- 1½ cups dark Jamaican rum
- 1 cup lemon juice
- ¾ cup dry gin
- ¾ cup brandy
- 4 to 6 10-ounce packages frozen sliced strawberries, thawed (depends on desired sweetness)

In large bowl, combine water and instant iced tea mix; stir until dissolved. Add bourbon, claret, orange juice, rum, lemon juice, gin, and brandy. Place sliced strawberries, one package at a time, in container of blender and mix at high speed until well blended. Add blended berries to instant iced tea mixture. Let stand, covered, several hours to ripen. Serve in a 1-gallon punch bowl over a large ice ring. Garnish with large strawberries, if desired. Makes approximately 45 to 50 4-ounce servings.

JOHN BULL HOT BUTTERED TEA SARONNO

2 ounces Amaretto di Saronno	2 tablespoons corn syrup
1 spiral lemon peel	2 tablespoons cider or apple jack, warm
1 stick cinnamon	1 cup tea, boiling
2 cloves	1 tablespoon butter

Place Amaretto, lemon peel, syrup, cinnamon, clove, and cider in a heatproof glass or mug. Add tea and float butter on top.

THE "ALPS" WINTER WARM-UP

4 cups water	½ cup heavy cream, whipped
½ cup instant iced-tea mix	
2 tablespoons anisette	Grated lemon rind

In large saucepan, combine water and instant iced tea mix; bring to boil. Remove from heat; stir in anisette. Pour into mugs. Top each with 2 measuring tablespoons whipped cream. Garnish with lemon rind. Makes 8 4-ounce servings.

LADY RAMSBOTTOM'S SPICY TEA TODDY

1 cup tea	1 tablespoon lemon juice
1 stick cinnamon	2 tablespoons orange juice
2 whole cloves	2 tablespoons corn syrup
1 large twist orange peel	2 ounces vodka

Heat first four ingredients in saucepan. Mix the remaining ingredients in a heatproof glass until thoroughly blended. Fill glass with spiced tea mixture and garnish with cinnamon stick and spiral of orange peel. If desired, top with orange flower water.

CHINSTRAP'S LOVE PUNCH

3 quarts cider
4 pints rum
8 cloves
4 pints Amaretto di Saronno
4 tablespoons sugar

1 lemon
1 orange
1 teaspoon ground cinnamon
1 teaspoon ground ginger

Peel the rind from the fruit in thin strips and chop the rind finely. Slice fruit. Put ½ pint cider in a small saucepan. Add sugar and spices. Cover and simmer for 30 minutes. Pour the rest of the cider into a large saucepan. Add the strained fruit and spice liquid. Heat slowly to a comfortable drinking temperature. Add the rum and Amaretto. Stir and heat once more. (Never overheat any alcohol mixture, otherwise its power will disappear.) Taste. Add more sugar if needed. Serves 10 to 12.

ENGLISH BISHOP

1 whole orange
6 cloves
3 tablespoons corn syrup
1 cup tea

1 cup tawny port
2 ounces dry Jamaican or Barbados rum

Stick cloves in orange, place on a flat heatproof dish, pour over it 2 tablespoons syrup, and brown it lightly in a medium hot oven (350°- 375°). Quarter the orange and place in a saucepan with 1 tablespoon syrup, the tea, and the port. Simmer it for 15 minutes and ladle into 4 punch cups. Heat rum, ignite it, and float ½ ounce of rum on each cup.

BLAZING TEE

4 ounces gin, warmed
4 ounces strong tea, boiling
1 spiral lemon peel

2 tablespoons lemon juice, stirred with
2 tablespoons corn syrup

Have ready two warmed heat-proof mugs with handles. Place boiling tea in one and warmed gin in the other. Ignite gin and while it blazes pour back and forth from one mug to the other. Add lemon-and-syrup mixture and serve with lemon peel.

TOWER BRIDGE HOT TEA TODDY

3 cups boiling water
6 tablespoons sugar
4 rounded teaspoons instant tea mix with lemon

6 tablespoons rum, bourbon, or brandy

In 1 quart pitcher, combine boiling water, sugar, and instant tea mix with lemon. Stir until dissolved. Add rum, bourbon, or brandy. Serve hot. Makes 4 6-ounce servings.

B & B TEA

Use stemmed glasses and be sure to place spoon in glass before pouring in hot tea. For each serving, pour 6 ounces (¾ cup) freshly brewed hot tea into 8-ounce glass. Add 1 jigger (1½-ounce) B & B liqueur. *Do not stir.* Top with lightly whipped cream or whipped topping. Sip through cream.

PARADISE ICED DESSERT TEA

1 1.7-ounce package   ¼ cup Grand Marnier
  (¼ cup) iced tea mix   4 scoops lemon sherbet
2 cups ice water

    In 1½-quart pitcher, combine iced tea mix, water, and Grand Marnier. Mix until dissolved. Pour into 4 parfait glasses. Top each with scoop of lemon sherbet. Allow a few minutes for sherbet to soften before serving. Makes about 4 4-ounce servings.

CLUB BLAZER LEMON COOLER

2 1.7-ounce packages   1 12 ounce bottle
  (½ cup) iced tea mix   ginger ale
3 cups water   Crushed ice
1 cup Galliano   1 lemon, thinly sliced

    In 2-quart pitcher, combine iced tea mix and water. Stir in Galliano. Chill in refrigerator until ready to serve. Before serving, add ginger ale and ice. Garnish each glass with lemon slice, if desired. Makes 10 4-ounce servings.

TEATOTALER—TALLY HO!

6 cups cold water   1½ cups light dry rum
1 cup instant iced tea mix

    In 2-quart pitcher, combine water and instant iced tea mix. Stir in rum. Serve over ice. Garnish with lemon slices. Makes 8 8-ounce servings.

GUNGA DIN FRUIT COOLER

3 cups cold water
1½ cups grapefruit juice
6 tablespoons sugar
6 tablespoons light rum
  or Mandarine
  Napoléon Liqueur

5 tablespoons instant tea
Assorted small pieces
  fruit (pineapple cubes,
  maraschino cherries, etc.)

In 2-quart pitcher, combine water, grapefruit juice, sugar, rum, or liqueur and instant tea. Mix until sugar and instant tea are dissolved. In each individual cube section of an ice tray, put one piece of fruit (toothpicks may be added to fruit, if desired). Freeze tray until tea cubes are firm (about 2 hours). Chill remaining tea mixture in refrigerator. Serve tea in tall glasses with fruited tea cubes. Makes about 4 8-ounce servings.

THE SAMOVAR TEASER

1½ quarts iced tea
6 ounces frozen orange
  juice, undiluted

6 ounces frozen lime juice
  undiluted
1 quart vodka

Using 1½ quarts of iced tea, add orange juice, lime juice, and stir. Add 1 quart vodka and blend well. Serve over ice.

THE COCKNEY WINE FROSTER

1½ quarts iced tea
¾ cup sugar

¾ cup lemon juice
1 bottle chablis wine

Teatime

Using 1½ quarts of iced tea, add sugar and stir to dissolve. Add lemon juice and bottle of chablis. Serve over crushed ice with fresh mint garnish.

MINTED "YOU & ME" FRAPPÉ

2 cups water
¼ cup instant tea mix
¼ cup confectioners sugar
¼ cup white creme de menthe
¼ cup white creme de cacao

In large bowl, combine water, instant tea mix, confectioners sugar, white creme de menthe, and white creme de cacao. Mix well. Pour into ice cube tray. Freeze until just frozen (about 2 hours). Scoop frozen mixture into large bowl or container of blender. Beat with electric mixer or blend in blender container at high speed until slushy. Serve immediately. Garnish with mint leaf, if desired. Makes about 4 5-ounce servings.

THE PEKING-ORANGE PEKOE COOLER

2 tablespoons orange juice
1 tablespoon lemon juice
2 tablespoons unsweetened pineapple juice
3 tablespoons corn syrup
3 ounces dry gin, vodka, or dry rum
½ teaspoon egg white
1 dash orange bitters
½ cup strong tea

Place all ingredients in cocktail shaker with crushed ice. Shake well and strain into tall glass over 3 ice cubes. Garnish with orange slice and pineapple stick (or mint).

TEA AMBASSADOR

2 ounces tea
2 ounces vodka or gin
2 tablespoons lemon juice
2 tablespoons corn syrup
2 tablespoons Kirsch

Place tea, vodka, lemon juice, syrup, and 1 tablespoon Kirsch in cocktail shaker with crushed ice. Shake well, strain into wineglass, and float remaining Kirsch on top.

SIR FRANCIS

½ cup strong tea
2 ounces gin or vodka
2 ounces lime juice
2 ounces grapefruit juice
2 tablespoons corn syrup

Place all ingredients in container of electric blender with lots of crushed ice. Blend until mixture forms a soft mush, like a frozen daiquiri. Serve garnished with lime slice.

Recipes for Afternoon Tea

It was an Englishman, John Montagu, Earl of Sandwich (1718-92), that brought about the invention of the sandwich. The Earl in his day was a passionate card player who never allowed himself time to eat. His considerate butler would serve him platefuls of meat and fish, sliced and put between slices of bread. Henceforth, the "sandwich" spread.

Teatime

FINGER SANDWICHES

Lay out slices of bread, toasted and buttered lightly if desired. Serve with the following choices of spread and garnish (or substitute your own favorites):

Thinly sliced ham with parsley or thinly sliced cucumber or radish
Sliced cold chicken and thinly sliced cucumber
Smoked salmon and red pepper with small slice of lemon
Thinly sliced cucumber
Cheddar cheese with thinly sliced stuffed green olive or tomato, or parsley
Watercress

Add salt, pepper, or mustard to taste. Close sandwiches, remove crusts, and slice each sandwich lengthwise into three or four "fingers" or squares.

OTHER TEA ACCOMPANIMENTS

Lemon Curd
Jams or jellies—usually a choice of three in small pots
Toasted muffins, crumpets, scones, or fingers of toast (toast bread lightly and cut off crusts)
Brandied Seed Cake
Jam Tarts
Assorted afternoon tea biscuits

CRUMPETS

Crumpets are a small, flat, breadlike cake somewhat similar to what the Americans call an English Muffin. The British variety is thinner and spongier than the American version. Crumpets are traditionally served in the old country with afternoon tea, as is, or toasted and accompanied with unsalted butter, jams, jellies, marmalades, or syrups.

1 cup flour
½ ounce (1 package) yeast
2 ounces butter
¼ teaspoon salt
1 tablespoon melted butter

2 tablespoons lukewarm water
1 egg
½ cup milk

Dissolve the yeast in the lukewarm water. Mix flour and salt together. Make a hole in the middle of the flour and add the yeast, egg, butter, and milk. Mix well. Cover and stand to rise for one hour or until double in size. Brush some crumpet rings with melted butter and put them in a greased, 10-inch frying pan. Place pan over moderate heat. Then drop one tablespoon of the batter into each ring. Turn the crumpets over and brown the other side. Grease a little more if they stick or burn. Butter them and serve hot.

You can also cook them in a 425° oven. Heat baking pan. Brush it over with melted butter. Repeat, as in frying pan. Turn them when holes have formed on the surface, and bake for another five minutes. Serves 10.

NOTE: If you do not have crumpet rings, use cookie cutters and grease inside surfaces.

SCONES

4 cups sifted cake flour or 3½ cups sifted all-purpose flour
4½ teaspoons double-acting baking powder
2 teaspoons sugar
1 teaspoon salt
½ cup butter or margarine
4 eggs, well beaten
⅔ cup light cream
2 teaspoons water

Sift flour, baking powder, sugar, and salt together into mixing bowl. Cut butter into dry material until the size of very tiny peas. Measure 4 tablespoons of beaten egg into a small cup; set aside. Beat cream into remaining beaten eggs. Make a "well" in flour mixture and pour in egg mixture. Stir together quickly, handling as little as possible. Place on lightly floured board. Pat with floured hands into a square ½-inch thick. With floured knife, cut into four squares; cut each square into four triangles. Transfer, with spatula, to ungreased baking sheets. Mix water with reserved beaten egg and brush over tops. Bake in very hot preheated oven (450°) for about 10 to 12 minutes or until golden brown. Serve hot.

BRANDIED SEED CAKE

1 17-ounce package pound cake mix	2 eggs
⅛ teaspoon nutmeg	1 tablespoon caraway seeds
½ cup milk	¼ cup brandy (*optional*)

Preheat oven to 325°. Pour cake mix into bowl; mix in nutmeg. Add milk; stir until well moistened. Beat about 1 minute at medium speed with electric mixer, or about 150 strokes by hand. Stir in eggs; beat 1 minute. Add seeds and brandy; stir in and beat 1 minute. Pour into ungreased 9- × 5- × 3-inch loaf pan. Bake in slow oven 1¼ hours or until golden brown and crust springs back when lightly touched with finger. Let cool in pan on rack for about 30 minutes. Loosen with spatula and return to rack for complete cooling.

ORANGE MARMALADE

Orange Marmalade is a "golden gift" given to us by the Scots and surely enjoyed by gourmets throughout the world.

It was during the eighteenth century that a Spanish ship carrying a cargo of Seville oranges and apples took shelter in the harbor of Dundee during a storm. Unfortunately, the storm did not abate, risking the life of the fruit. A Scotsman, James Keiller, bought the cargo at a bargain, but to his regret, no one would buy the bitter oranges and apples. His thrifty wife came to his rescue by making pots of jam and selling them. This was the first Dundee Marmalade! Its unique flavor is derived by making the marmalade in old sherry barrels that once matured sherry. Then they are used by distillers to age scotch, and only after that are they suitable for ripening Dundee Marmalade! It's a must with English muffins, scones, or crumpets.

To make about 4 pints:

2 large Valencia oranges *8 cups sugar, preferably*
2 large lemons *superfine*
2½ to 3 quarts cold water

Wash fruit and pat dry with paper towels. Cut fruit into quarters and remove piths. Soak the fruit in water for 24 hours. Remove fruit, and cut pulp and peel into thin strips. Return pulp and peel to the soaking water. Bring to a boil over high heat. Reduce heat to low, stirring occasionally; simmer uncovered for 2 hours. Add sugar; stir thoroughly and bring to a boil over moderate heat. Continue to boil briskly until the mixture reaches 220° on a candy thermometer. Remove from heat. Cool 10 minutes, then spoon into sterilized jars and seal. To prevent peel from floating to the top, shake the jars as they cool.

LEMON CURD

4 eggs
Pinch salt
2 cups sugar
½ cup lemon juice

¼ cup butter, room temperature
2 tablespoons lemon rind, grated

Beat eggs; add salt. Stir in sugar, butter, lemon juice, and grated rind. Blend well. Cook in top of double-boiler for 30 minutes. Stir occasionally until thickened and smooth. Cool at room temperature; store in refrigerator. Delicious on toast, scones, biscuits, etc. May also be used as a tart filling.

RASPBERRY OR STRAWBERRY JAM

6 cups raspberries or strawberries
4 cups sugar
⅓ cup lemon juice

Wash the berries. Dry them well and place in a heavy pot. Cover berries with sugar and place pot over low heat. Stir the mixture gently with wooden spoon until mixture becomes juicy. Raise heat to moderate and cease stirring. When mixture is bubbling, set timer for 15 minutes. After 15 minutes, tilt the pot to see if the liquid on the bottom has a tendency to set. If not, boil a little longer. Sprinkle with lemon juice and allow to cool. Stir berries gently. Pour into jars and seal. Makes 3 16-ounce jars.

Recipes for High Tea or Light Supper

WELSH RAREBIT

1 cup grated cheddar
   cheese
4 tablespoons beer
2 tablespoons butter
¼ teaspoon salt, pepper

1 egg yolk
1 teaspoon Dijon
   mustard
2 slices of trimmed toast

Stir cheese and beer over low heat until cheese melts. Add salt, pepper, mustard, and butter. After butter has melted, add slightly beaten yolk. Spoon over toast and quickly brown under broiler. Serves 2.

BANGERS AND MASH

8 pork sausages
6 cooked potatoes
¼ cup milk
2 tablespoons butter
¼ cup grated cheese

Salt and pepper, to taste
Nutmeg, dash
1 onion, sliced and
   separated into rings

Brown sausages in skillet, drain. Mash potatoes with milk, butter, cheese, seasonings, and nutmeg. Place half of mixture in buttered casserole; arrange bangers on potatoes and cover with remaining mixture. Dot with butter and bake in 400° oven for 10 minutes. Meanwhile, deep fry onion rings in hot fat until golden, drain and arrange over dish. Serves 4.

MUSHROOMS ON ENGLISH MUFFINS

1 pound fresh
  mushrooms, sliced
2 tablespoons butter or
  margarine
1 2-ounce jar diced
  pimientos, drained
⅓ cup Amaretto di
  Saronno

1 cup dairy sour cream
1¼ teaspoons Worcester-
  shire sauce
Salt and freshly ground
  pepper to taste
Buttered, toasted English
  muffin halves

Sauté mushrooms in butter or margarine for 2 to 3 minutes. Add diced pimientos, Amaretto, dairy sour cream, Worcestershire sauce, salt, and freshly ground pepper. Continue cooking over low heat until mixture thickens. Serve on buttered, toasted English muffin halves. Makes 4 servings.

CORNISH PASTIES

1 pound beef (top or
  bottom round)
1 tablespoon butter
1 cup beef broth
2 onions, minced
2 potatoes, diced
½ teaspoon salt, pepper

1 tablespoon cornstarch
2 tablespoons water
1 egg yolk
1 tablespoon cream
Pie pastry (recipe for 6
  6-inch crusts)

Cut beef into small cubes; sauté in butter with onions until latter are limp, not brown. Add beef broth; cover and simmer 30 minutes. Add diced potatoes; simmer 10 minutes more. Roll out pastry into 6 6-inch circles. Using slotted spoon, place equal por-

Teatime

tions of meat on each circle. Thicken meat broth with a mixture of cornstarch and water. Divide sauce equally over meat portions. Dampen edges of pastry circles, fold in half, and seal edges by crimping with fork. Brush with egg yolk beaten with cream; place on buttered and floured cookie sheet and bake 35 minutes in preheated 350° oven. Serves 6.

FISH AND CHIPS

1½ lb. halibut, flounder, or cod
1½ cups flour
3 large Idaho potatoes
1 cup beer, water, or milk
2 eggs, beaten
Salt, pepper
Lemon juice
Paprika
Oil or shortening

Cut fish into serving pieces and sprinkle with lemon juice. Peel potatoes, cut into strips, and place into iced water. Make batter with 1 cup of the flour, beer, salt, pepper, and paprika, stirring with whisk until smooth. Drain potatoes and dry on paper towel. Deep-fry in 375° oil or shortening until tender, but not brown; drain on paper towel. Beat batter again, and stir in beaten eggs. Dredge fish in batter, and fry in same oil for 5 minutes; remove. Reheat oil to 375°, fry fish until crisp for another 4 or 5 minutes; remove, drain, and keep warm. Return chips to fryer for 4 to 5 minutes until golden brown; drain and sprinkle with salt. Wrap fish and chips in wax paper and newspaper, and sprinkle with malt vinegar. Serves 4.

SALMON FISH CAKES OR PATTIES

2 cups fine breadcrumbs
2 egg yolks
1 cup white sauce*
⅛ teaspoon grated nutmeg
Juice of 1 lemon
1¼ pound salmon, cooked and flaked
1 pound mushrooms, chopped
2 eggs well beaten
⅛ teaspoon paprika
¾ tablespoon butter
Pepper and salt to taste

Sauté the mushrooms in butter, add lemon, season lightly, cook until pan juices are almost not there. Heat the *white sauce* slowly, stir in egg yolks, and cook without bringing to a boil, until thickened. Season with salt, pepper, paprika, and nutmeg. Then, stir in the mushrooms and fold in the fish carefully to avoid crushing the flakes. Spread lightly on one sheet of buttered foil and cover with another. Chill.

Form into patties or croquettes, dip in egg and breadcrumbs, and fry in vegetable oil until golden brown and warm throughout. Serve on a dish garnished with parsley and sliced lemon. Serves 6.

*BASIC WHITE SAUCE (1 cup)

2 tablespoons butter
1½ to 2 tablespoons flour
1 cup milk
Small onion,
2 whole cloves,
1 small bay leaf

Combine the butter and flour and blend over low heat for 3 to 4 minutes, add 1 cup of milk, and slowly cook and stir. Then put in onion, studded with cloves and bay leaf, salt and pepper to taste, and stir with wire whisk or wooden spoon until it thickens and is smooth. Place in the oven at 350° and cook slowly for 20 minutes. Strain off seasoning and season sauce to taste.

BAKEWELL TART

Bakewell tarts originate from Bakewell, Derbyshire. The tart was intended for high tea and is, in fact, a cross between a cake and a pudding.

1 pound (4 cups) short or Rough Puff Pastry (recipe follows)
2 tablespoons strawberry jam
1 egg
4 tablespoons butter
4 tablespoons sugar
2 tablespoons self-rising flour
¾ cup glacé icing

Line 9-inch tin with the pastry. Work up the edges and spread the middle with jam. Cream together the butter and sugar. Add the egg and a little of the flour; beat well. Then add the rest of the flour. Spread the mixture over the jam. Bake at 350° for 20 to 30 minutes. When cold, pour the glacé icing over the top and allow to set. Serve cold. Serves 6.

GLACÉ ICING

2 cups confectioners sugar
1 tablespoon water
1 teaspoon lemon juice

Sieve confectioners sugar into saucepan, which already has water and lemon juice. Stir over low heat until sugar is melted. Pour over tart, allowing icing to run down the sides and smoothing it with a hot knife.

ROUGH PUFF PASTRY

2 cups sifted all-purpose flour
¼ teaspoon salt
¼ cup lard, chilled, cut into ¼-inch slices
¼ pound unsalted butter, chilled, cut into ¼-inch slices
4 to 6 tablespoons ice water

Sift flour and salt together in large, chilled mixing bowl. Add butter and lard and quickly rub the flour and fat together with your fingertips until the mixture looks like coarse meal. Pour 4 tablespoons ice water over mixture and collect the dough into a ball. If the dough crumbles, add up to 2 tablespoons more ice water, a teaspoon at a time, until dough adheres. Dust lightly with flour, wrap in wax paper, and chill for 30 minutes.

Place pastry on a lightly floured board and press into a rectangular shape, 1 inch thick. Dust with small amount of flour and roll into 21- × 6-inch strip. Fold the strip into thirds to form 3-layered rectangular packet. Turn the pastry around so that an open end faces you. Roll out again to 21- × 6-inch strip. Fold into thirds as before. Repeat entire process twice again, ending with pastry folded into a packet. (Rough going, but it is worth it!) Wrap the pastry tightly in wax paper, foil, or in a plastic bag and refrigerate 1 hour. Pastry may be kept in refrigerator up to 4 days before using.

Savories

Earliest references to the savory seem to be Victorian. It's an entirely English invention; it forms no part of any other cuisine. Its original purpose was to cleanse the palate after the delicious but cloying sweet, and prepare it, in the case of gentlemen, for the port. Ladies often missed the savory, their delicate Victorian appetites already sated on the dinner courses that preceeded it. Gentlemen, on the other hand, sometimes missed the sweet or dessert; this was considered discerning and manly. Today, a savory is sometimes offered instead of a dessert, as many people prefer not to conclude a meal on a sweet taste. Queen Victoria was extremely fond of marrow toasts, the marrow of which came from marrow bones that are very rarely served today. Her son, Edward VII, loved Canapes Diane, which are better known as Mushrooms on Toast.

Here are some of my favorite savories. Nowadays, savories are ideal for a light luncheon, high tea, a late supper, or an after-dinner snack. They go very well with tea, needless to say.

MUSHROOMS ON TOAST

1 6-ounce can mushroom caps, drained
1 tablespoon butter
6 slices hot buttered toast
Salt and freshly ground pepper

Gently heat the mushrooms in butter; keep hot. Cut each slice of toast into three strips. Arrange 3 mushrooms on each strip; sprinkle with salt and pepper. Makes about 6 servings.

SARDINES ON TOAST

1 3¾-ounce can sardines, drained
5 slices hot buttered toast
Half lemon
Cayenne pepper

Broil sardines a few seconds on each side, just enough to heat through. Cut each slice of toast into three strips and arrange a sardine on each. Sprinkle with lemon juice, then with cayenne. Makes about 5 servings.

SCOTCH WOODCOCK

4 eggs
Salt and pepper
3 tablespoons heavy cream
2 tablespoons butter
4 slices hot buttered toast
Anchovy paste

Beat eggs with salt, pepper, and cream. Scramble eggs in butter and cook just until done, still soft and moist. Spread anchovy paste on toast; top with scrambled eggs. Garnish with chives or parsley, if desired. Makes 4 servings.

ANGELS ON HORSEBACK

1 8-ounce can oysters, drained
10 slices bacon, cut in half
5 slices hot buttered toast

Wrap each oyster in a half slice of bacon; secure with toothpick. Broil until bacon is crisp. Cut each slice of toast into 4 squares and place an oyster on each. Makes 20 pieces.

DEVILS ON HORSEBACK

12 large prunes or black plums
1 bay leaf
1 cup dry red wine
6 slices bacon
¼ cup drained chutney, chopped
Watercress or parsley springs for garnish

Simmer prunes in wine with bay leaf until tender, about 15 minutes. Cool in wine; remove pits. Fill each prune with 1 teaspoon chutney. Wrap each prune with a half slice of bacon; secure with toothpick. Place in baking dish. Bake in preheated 400° oven until bacon is crisp, about 15 minutes. Drain on paper toweling. Serve garnished with watercress. Devils on Horseback may also be served on small squares of hot buttered toast. Makes 6 servings.

SCOTCH EGGS

1 pound sausage meat
½ teaspoon sage
½ teaspoon thyme
2 tablespoons minced parsley
½ cup flour
½ teaspoon salt
Pepper
8 hardboiled eggs
2 eggs, lightly beaten
1 cup breadcrumbs

Mix sausage meat with herbs and shape into eight round patties; wrap sausage patties around hardboiled eggs. Roll eggs in flour seasoned with salt and pepper, then in beaten eggs and in breadcrumbs. Deep fry in hot fat until sausage is cooked. May be served hot or cold in eight portions.

SHROPSHIRE HERB ROLL

PASTRY
2 cups flour
½ teaspoon salt
½ pound butter
6 tablespoons water

FILLING
2 tablespoons minced parsley
1 tablespoon minced chives
½ teaspoon each of chervil, marjoram, and thyme
1 minced onion
1 egg, lightly beaten
½ pound crisp fried bacon, crumbled
2 cups cold, chopped, cooked, chicken
1 egg yolk beaten with a little milk

SAUCE
1 tablespoon butter
1 tablespoon flour
½ cup beef broth
1 tablespoon Madeira

Sift flour and salt into bowl. Blend in butter with fingertips. Add just enough water to roll pastry into a ball. Cover with waxed paper and chill. Dust dough with flour and roll into rectangle 12 inches by 8 inches. Blend herbs and onion into beaten egg and spread over pastry. Sprinkle the bacon, chicken, salt, and pepper over this.

Melt tablespoon of butter and add flour. Gradually stir in broth to form a very thick sauce. Flavor with Madeira. Pour over bacon and chicken mix and roll up pastry like a jelly roll, pinching in ends to contain the sauce.

Place on a buttered and floured cooked sheet, brush with milk and egg yolk, and bake in a 400° oven for 15 minutes. Reduce heat to 350° and bake for 30 minutes until it is golden brown. Serves four.

KIPPER PASTE

½ cup clarified butter
4 smoked kippers
4 teaspoons anchovy paste
Ground cloves, mace, cayenne to taste
½ cup softened butter (more, if needed)

Cover kippers with water and simmer for 5 minutes. Drain and fillet, discarding skin, tails, backbones, and roe. Place in blender and blend with remaining ingredients until smooth and creamy. Add more butter if too dry. Spoon into serving dish, pour clarified butter over it to seal paste. Refrigerate until firm. Serve on thinly sliced toasted white bread. Makes about 2 cups.

GAMMON RASHERS BOXTY

From Ireland (Donegal). Traditionally eaten on the eve of All Saints' Day.

3 cups peeled and grated potatoes
1 cup flour
Salt to taste
2 tablespoons butter
4 tablespoons milk (more, if needed)
6 thick rashers of lean bacon

Grill bacon and drain on paper towel and reserve. Squeeze potatoes as dry as possible and combine with flour and salt. Gradually add just enough milk to hold mixture together. Let stand for 1 hour. Melt butter in a very hot, 9-inch skillet. Spread batter into skillet and cook over medium heat until underside is golden brown. Turn pancake and brown other side. Serve with reserved bacon rashers. Serves 4.

Cooking With Tea

TEA EGGS—CHINESE STYLE

Ideal for cocktail parties! And for dieting! The ingredients seep through the cracked eggs, giving a unique taste and appearance. Store in their liquid in the refrigerator.

1 dozen eggs
3 tablespoons soy sauce
2 tablespoons salt
3 tablespoons tea
1 star anise

Boil eggs until hard; place in cold water to cool. On a smooth surface, roll the eggs until cracks appear all around the shell. Do not remove shell. Place cracked eggs, and all other ingredients, in a pot. Add water to cover eggs. Bring to boil, then simmer for 1 hour. Serve hot or cold.

TEA WITH EGGS

This nourishing tea brew is a European version of Tibetan buttered tea, which is made with salt, not sugar. To quote Sir Kenelme Digbie, 1669. "This for when you come home from attending business abroad, and are very hungry and yet have not conveniency to eat, presently, a competent meal."

2 teaspoons of your choice of tea, or 2 teabags
2½ cups water
2 egg yolks
Sugar to taste
Grated nutmeg to taste

Teatime

Pour fresh boiled water onto the tea and brew to taste. Then, pour through tea strainer into a blender. Add egg yolks, sugar, and nutmeg (grated to taste) and blend for a few seconds. Drink while still hot. You can add white wine if desired. Serves 2.

Festivi-Teas

TEA PARTY PUFFS

½ *cup butter or margarine*
1 *cup boiling water*
½ *teaspoon salt*
1 *cup sifted all purpose flour*
4 *eggs, unbeaten*

Preheat oven to 400°. Put butter into medium saucepan, add boiling water, and heat over high heat until butter is melted. Turn heat low, add salt and flour together, and stir vigorously until mixture leaves sides of pan in a smooth, compact ball, about 2 minutes. Remove from heat. Add eggs, one at a time, beating with a spoon until smooth after each addition. After adding last egg, beat until mixture has a satinlike sheen. Drop mixture by teaspoons—1½ inches apart—on greased cookie sheet, shaping each into a mound that points up in the center. Bake 20 to 25 minutes without opening oven. Puffs should be puffed and golden. Remove with spatula to wire rack to cool. Split puffs almost all the way around, or slice off top. Fill with your choice of filling and replace tops; puffs may be made in advance and frozen unfilled. Fillings you will enjoy include whipped cream, fruit, chocolate whip, custard, preserves, and lemon curd. Makes 3 to 3½ dozen puffs.

CHEESE STRAWS

4 tablespoons butter, softened
4 tablespoons finely grated sharp cheese
¾ cup unsifted all-purpose flour
⅛ teaspoon cayenne pepper
¼ teaspoon salt
1 egg yolk
2 tablespoons cold water

Cream butter and cheese together. Blend in flour, cayenne, and salt. Mix egg yolk with water and stir into flour mixture. Form dough into a rectangle about 1-inch thick. Chill in waxed paper for 1 hour or more. Place dough on floured surface and roll into long rectangle ¼-inch thick and about 3 inches wide. With a sharp knife, cut the dough into ½-inch wide strips. Place on ungreased cookie sheet and bake in preheated 400° oven until golden, about 15 minutes. Cool on wire rack. Makes about 2 dozen.

LOW-CALORIE CHEESE DIP

1 8-ounce cup cottage cheese
1 tablespoon lemon juice
¼ teaspoon salt
3 tablespoons minced dill pickle
1 tablespoon pickle juice
¼ teaspoon paprika

Press cottage cheese through a sieve. Add other ingredients and blend well. Refrigerate until needed. Use as a dip for potato chips or fresh vegetables (carrot sticks, cauliflower and broccoli flowerettes, radishes, cucumber). Makes about 1¼ cups.

FESTIVE CHEESE DIP

1 3-ounce package cream cheese, softened
1 2-ounce can anchovy fillets, drained
2 cups 16-ounce small-curd cottage cheese
½ cup chopped ripe olives
2 teaspoons chopped pimiento
2 teaspoons chopped chives

Combine cream cheese and anchovies; mix until smooth. Stir in cottage cheese, olives, pimiento, and chives. Turn into serving dish and, if desired, garnish with parsley sprig. Serve with raw celery sticks, cherry tomatoes, cauliflower, cucumbers, and mushrooms. Makes about 2⅔ cups.

SHERRIED CHICKEN LIVER PATE

1½ pounds chicken livers
1½ teaspoons anchovy paste
6 strips crisply cooked bacon, minced
1 tablespoon grated onion
2 tablespoons minced parsley
¼ teaspoon pepper
⅓ cup chopped pistachio nuts or blanched chopped almonds
½ teaspoon well-rubbed dried oregano
¾ teaspoon well-rubbed dried basil
3 tablespoons butter, melted
3 tablespoons pale dry cocktail sherry

Simmer livers until tender. Drain and mash well with fork or put through a grinder. Blend thoroughly with remaining ingredients. Pack into a mold or pile into a serving dish. Cover and chill. Makes 12 servings.

SESAME CHEESE STICKS

1 pound sharp cheddar cheese, grated or shredded
¼ pound butter, creamed
½ cup toasted sesame seeds*

2 cups sifted all-purpose flour
½ teaspoon salt
¼ teaspoon cayenne pepper

Blend cheese and butter; stir in sesame seeds. Sift together flour, salt, and pepper; blend with first mixture. (This is quite a stiff mixture.) Pinch off pieces of dough and roll with hand into long pencil shapes about ¾ inch in diameter. Place one inch apart on ungreased cookie sheet. Bake in preheated moderate oven (350°) for about 15 minutes. Do not allow sticks to brown.

*Place seeds in a shallow baking pan in preheated moderate oven (350°) for about 20 minutes. Stir several times for uniform coloring. Makes 12 to 14 servings.

DEVILED HAM ROLL-UPS

1 cup prepared biscuit mix
⅓ cup milk
1 teaspoon dry mustard

1 4½-ounce can deviled ham spread
2 tablespoons sweet pickle relish, drained

Place mix in bowl, add milk, and stir with fork to a soft dough. Beat vigorously, about 20 strokes, until stiff but sticky. Turn onto a floured pastry cloth and knead about 8 to 10 times. Roll dough into a rectangle, about 9" × 13". Blend together deviled ham, pickle relish, and mustard. Spread on biscuit dough. Roll up from long side. Cut crosswise into pinwheels about ¾-inch thick. Place pinwheels one-inch apart on ungreased baking sheet. Bake in very hot oven (450°) about 10 minutes or until biscuit is golden brown. Cool thoroughly on rack. Makes about 16 pieces.

QUICHE LORRAINE

1 9 inch-unbaked pie shell, well chilled	¾ teaspoon salt Pinch nutmeg
1 tablespoon soft butter	Pinch sugar
12 slices bacon	Pinch cayenne
4 eggs, beaten	⅛ teaspoon white pepper
2 cups heavy cream	¼ pound natural Swiss
2 dashes Tabasco sauce	cheese, grated (1 cup)

Preheat oven to 425°. Rub butter over pie shell. Fry bacon until crisp. Drain. Crumble into small pieces. Combine eggs, cream, tabasco, salt, nutmeg, sugar, cayenne, and pepper. With hand beater, beat just enough to mix thoroughly. Sprinkle bacon and grated cheese into pie shell. Pour in cream mixture. Bake at 425° for 15 minutes. Reduce heat to 300° and bake 40 minutes, or until silver knife inserted in center comes out clean. Let stand about 15 minutes or more before cutting into wedges. Makes 6 to 8 servings.

LOBSTER QUICHE

- 1 9-ounce package lobster tails
- 1 9-inch uncooked pastry shell
- 3 3-ounce packages cream cheese, at room temperature
- ¾ cup heavy cream
- 3 egg yolks
- 2 eggs
- ½ teaspoon salt
- ⅛ teaspoon white pepper
- 1 tablespoon grated onion
- ½ teaspoon dried dill weed

Parboil lobster by dropping into boiling salted water. When water reboils, remove from heat, drain, and cover with cold water to cool quickly. Remove shell and membrane from lobster and cut meat into small cubes. Sprinkle evenly over bottom of pie shell; set aside. Blend cheese with cream until smooth. Beat egg yolks and eggs together. Add salt, pepper, grated onion, dill weed, and pour over diced lobster. Bake in preheated hot oven (400°) for about 30 minutes, or until firm, puffy, and golden. Cool on a rack for at least 10 minutes before cutting. Cut into 12 wedges for equal number of servings.

STUFFED MUSHROOMS

- 24 fresh mushrooms, about 1½ inches in diameter
- 2 3-ounce packages cream cheese, at room temperature
- 2 4½-ounce cans deviled ham
- ¼ cup minced green pepper
- 2 tablespoons minced onion
- ¼ teaspoon well-rubbed dried marjoram
- Red vegetable color, optional
- Parsley

Wash mushrooms and dry. Remove stems and save for some other purpose. Place mushroom caps, top side down, on shallow tray. Blend remaining ingredients, except parsley. Add color if desired. Fill caps with mixture. Cover with foil or plastic and chill. When ready to serve top each with a small sprig of parsley. Makes 12 servings.

APPLE CHEESE FLAN

1 egg
⅓ cup sugar
¼ cup unsifted flour
½ cup heavy cream
2 tablespoons brandy
1 9-inch pie crust, unbaked

½ teaspoon cinnamon
2-ounce (½ cup) shredded Norwegian cheese
4 medium eating or baking apples
⅓ cup firmly packed brown sugar

In small bowl, combine egg and sugar; beat until thick and lemon-colored. Gradually beat in flour. Stir in heavy cream and brandy. Pour custard mixture into unbaked pie crust. Sprinkle Norwegian cheese over top. Quarter, core, and peel apples; slice each quarter into thirds. Arrange apple slices in attractive pattern on top of cheese. In small bowl, combine brown sugar and cinnamon; mix thoroughly. Sprinkle brown sugar mixture over top of apples. Bake in preheated 400° oven for 40 minutes.

HAM SALAD IN HONEYDEW RINGS

2 cups cooked, diced lean ham
¾ cup diced celery
2 3-ounce cans sliced mushrooms, drained
⅓ cup mayonnaise
1 teaspoon dry mustard
1 honeydew melon, chilled
Boston or Bibb lettuce
Lemon wedges
Parsley

Mix together ham, celery, and mushrooms; cover and chill. When ready to serve, mix mayonnaise with dry mustard and combine with ham mixture. Cut four rings, about 1-inch wide, from center of melon. (Save ends of melon to eat as such or use in a fresh fruit cup the next day.) Discard seeds and peel rings. Place on lettuce. Pile salad onto rings. Garnish with lemon wedges and a sprig of parsley. Makes 4 servings.

PARSLEY ASPIC WITH HAM

3 envelopes unflavored gelatin
¾ cup cold water
5 tablespoons chicken-flavored instant bouillon
3¼ cups boiling water
2 cups minced parsley
¼ teaspoon dried tarragon, well rubbed
½ teaspoon celery seed
2 tablespoons cider vinegar
3 cups finely diced lean ham

Sprinkle gelatin over cold water and set aside to soften. Stir bouillon into boiling water, add softened gelatin, and stir until dissolved. Sprinkle in tarragon and celery seed. Cool. Stir in vinegar. Chill, stirring occasionally, until mixture reaches consistency of un-

Teatime

beaten egg white. Stir in ham cubes and parsley, mixing well. Pour into lightly oiled 9- × 5- × 3-inch loaf pan or into mold holding about 6 cups. Chill until form. Unmold on serving plate and garnish with egg slices or wedges. Makes 6 to 8 servings.

Pies

**Simple Simon met a pieman going to the fair.
Said Simple Simon to the pieman, "Let me taste your ware."
Said the pieman to Simple Simon, "Show me first your penny."
Said Simple Simon to the pieman, "Sir, I haven't any."**

Traveling piemen sold meat pies all over England until very recent times. Pies sold in this manner were meant to be topped off with aspic or butter forced through a vent in the crust after baking. This method of sealing kept air from reaching the filling of the pie. This kept the pie from spoiling before it was sold. *Can you imagine, some piemen didn't top off their pies and sometimes poisoned customers. Some disaster! No ideas, now!* "Simple Simon" began as a warning (about piemen) to mid-eighteenth century housewives.

Nowhere else, as in Britain, from the Middle Ages to the nineteenth century, did the meat pie reach such a high degree of perfection. It was the original convenience food, having evolved as a way to eat meat in gravy before the fork came into general use. The medieval meat pie, very rich and full of delicious tidbits, was a feast day dish. Whatever its main ingredients (meat, fowl, or fish) it also contained three or four of the following: coxcomb, artichoke bottoms, truffles, plums, dates, currants, apples, pears, orange or lemon peel, herbs, and spices.

A common combination, as late as the mid-seventeenth century, was larks, sparrows, and oysters mixed with chestnuts, dates, and pickled barberries, all moistened with egg.

People in the Middle Ages enjoyed many combinations such as this, and enjoyed meat and fish sweetened, as well as seasoned mainly with salt. By the end of the seventeenth century, however, the division between sweet and savory seems to have become accepted. Fewer and fewer sweets were called for in pie recipes.

This may have been due, in part, to a relaxation in the observance of fast days, since such combinations of meat and fruit may have been originally devised to conceal meat which was eaten during Lent.

Another reason that the meat or game pie began to lose its importance was the growing popularity of the potato. It gradually made meat with pastry redundant. Sometimes potatoes are served with pie, but a pie's real point is that it is complete and needs no accompaniment.

The two types of pies that remain popular in Britain are factory-made and for sale in pubs, canteens, and grocery stores. They are the steak or chicken pie, and the pork or veal pie with ham and eggs.

One finds them in pubs. They go down to your "Aunty Nelly" (belly) very well with a tankard of ale or a good "cuppa."

STEAK AND KIDNEY PIE

½ Rough Puff Pastry recipe (see page 131)
2 pounds lean chuck or sirloin of beef in 1-inch cubes
4 cubed veal kidneys
3 tablespoons oil
3 minced onions
2 tablespoons flour
1 cup beef stock
½ cup red wine
Salt and Pepper
1 tablespoon Worcestershire sauce
1 bay leaf
1 egg yolk beaten with 1 tablespoon milk

Make Rough Puff Pastry and chill. Brown beef and kidneys in hot oil. Add onions and cook for 5 minutes. Stir in flour, beef broth, and wine. Add salt, pepper, Worcestershire sauce and bay leaf. Cover and simmer **for** 1½ hours. Roll out dough ¼-inch thick. Transfer steak and kidney mixture to a baking dish and cover with pastry. Cut gashes in center of pastry to let steam escape. Brush with milk and egg yolk and bake in 350° oven for 35 minutes. Serves 6.

COTTAGE PIE

2 pounds ground lamb
1 tablespoon oil
1 tablespoon butter
2 minced onions
2 minced garlic cloves
3 diced carrots
2 tomatoes, peeled, seeded, and chopped
1 teaspoon tomato paste
1 tablespoon flour
1 cup beef broth
½ teaspoon rosemary
1 cup cooked green beans
Salt and pepper
6 potatoes, boiled and mashed
1 tablespoon melted butter

Brown lamb in hot oil and drain off rendered fat. Melt butter and cook onions and garlic until soft. Add carrots and cook for five minutes. Stir in flour and tomato paste. Add tomatoes, beef broth, rosemary, green beans, and ground lamb. Season with salt and pepper. Place in a baking dish, top with mashed potatoes, and brush with melted butter. Bake in a 350° oven for 30 minutes. Serves 6.

SHEPHERD'S PIE

Eat it while shepherds watch their flocks.

2 cups cooked lamb, chopped
2 tablespoons butter
2 minced onions
2 minced carrots
Salt and pepper
Thyme, mace, nutmeg
2 tablespoons flour, dissolved with a little cold water
2 cups beef broth
1 cup cooked carrots, in 1-inch pieces
1 cup small, cooked potato cubes
½ cup cooked parsnips, in 1-inch pieces
5 potatoes, boiled and mashed
1 tablespoon melted butter

Heat butter and cook the minced onion and carrot. Add lamb and seasonings and cook until heated through. Stir in flour, add beef broth and cook 20 minutes, stirring occasionally, until sauce thickens. Turn into a buttered baking dish and add the cooked carrots, potato cubes, and parsnips. Top with mashed potatoes, dot with melted butter, and bake in a 350° oven until top is browned. Serves 6.

COLONEL CHINSTRAP'S COLD CHICKEN PIE

This is a version that I have adapted from Mrs. Anne Blencowe's Chicken Pye (1694) and Gervase Markham's Chicken Pye (1615). It's very simple to make and absolutely devastating!

¾ pound Rough Puff Pastry (see page 131)
6 cold boiled chicken breasts
2½ pints double cream, whipped
½ pound mushrooms
3 hard-boiled eggs
2 ounces tongue or ham
½ teaspoon salt
½ teaspoon pepper
2 tablespoons wine vinegar
Fresh tarragon, mint, or parsley

Line a pie dish with the pastry and crimp the edges. Line with foil and fill with uncooked rice. Prebake at 400° for 8 to 10 minutes. Remove foil and rice and cool to room temperature. Take the chicken breasts and remove the skin. Rub with salt, pepper, sage, tarragon, and wine vinegar. Prepare hard-boiled eggs. Peel and quarter mushrooms. Slice and sauté tongue or ham, cut in thin julienne strips. Whip the cream and spoon a portion into the bottom of a pie dish. Arrange the chicken breasts as desired on top of the cream and then sprinkle the ham or tongue, mushrooms, and eggs over the chicken. Take the rest of the cream and whip with fresh mint, tarragon, or parsley and a little lemon juice. Now cover the dish. Serves 6.

HADDOCK PIE

6 boiled potatoes
4 tablespoons butter
½ cup milk
Salt, pepper and nutmeg
1 pound haddock, cooked and flaked
1 dozen cooked shrimp
3 tablespoons butter
2 onions, peeled and sliced

3 tablespoons flour
1 cup milk
1 cup heavy cream
3 tablespoons chopped parsley
2 teaspoons anchovy paste
2 tablespoons melted butter

Mash potatoes with 4 tablespoons butter and ½ cup milk. Season with salt, pepper, and nutmeg. Cook sliced onion in melted butter until soft. Stir in flour, milk, and cream and cook, stirring constantly with a whisk, until smooth and thick. Add parsley and anchovy paste and mix in thoroughly. Gently fold in haddock and shrimp, season to taste and pour into baking dish. Spread mashed potatoes over top, brush with melted butter, and bake in 400° oven for 20 minutes. If desired, brown under broiler. Serves 4 to 6.

PORK AND APPLE PIE

In the Middle Ages, meat was often cooked into pies with fruit and spices. Meat may have been hidden in this way, during periods of fasting, from the eyes of the overzealous. Meat and fruit, and meat and sweets, were a familiar combination to the early Britons, since they made no distinction at all between spices and sugar. Sugar was just one more spice!

4 pounds lean pork diced
2 cups minced onions
Salt, pepper, sage to taste
4 tart green apples, peeled cored, and diced
½ cup water or cider
2 pounds boiled potatoes
4 tablespoons butter
½ cup milk
2 tablespoons melted butter

Butter an ovenproof casserole. Spread ⅓ of the diced pork over the bottom and sprinkle with ½ cup of the minced onion. Season with salt, pepper, and sage. Top this with half the apples and another half cup of onion. Season again, and repeat with layers of pork, onions, and apples. Add seasoning and top with the remaining pork. Pour in the water and bring to a boil over high heat. Cover casserole and bake in a 325° oven for 1½ hours. Mash the potatoes with 4 tablespoons of butter, the milk, salt, and pepper. When pork is done, spread the mashed potatoes over it and brush with melted butter. Bake for 10 minutes until top browns. Serves 8 to 10.

MELTON MOWBRAY PIE

Melton Mowbray Pork Pie dates from the fourteenth century when it included raisins and currants. It was later intended for high teas and also served to returning members of hunting parties. Every county, and every house, farm, and inn in each county, had its own recipe for Melton Mowbray Pork Pie.

4 pounds pork shoulder *1 minced onion*
1 pig's foot *½ cup dry white wine,*
1 sliced onion *cider, or water*
Salt, pepper, thyme *½ cup melted butter*
1 Rough Puff Pastry *1 egg beaten with*
recipe (see page 131) *1 tablespoon milk*

Bone and trim pork shoulder. Dice meat. Place bones together with pig's foot, sliced onion, salt, pepper, and thyme in a kettle and cover with water. Bring to boil and simmer slowly for 3 hours. Prepare pastry, and line a buttered loaf pan or spring form with ½ of the dough. Fill with the diced meat, minced onion, salt, pepper, and thyme to taste. Pour in wine or cider and melted butter. Cover with top crust, moisten, and crimp the edges together. Cut a hole in the center of the crust and bake in a 300° oven for 2 hours. Thirty minutes before the pie is done, brush with beaten egg and milk. Strain the pork broth, skim off fat, and reduce over high heat to 2 cups. Pour hot broth through a funnel into the hole in the top. Refrigerate until aspic is set. Serves 6 to 8.

VEAL AND HAM PIE

Traditionally, veal and ham pies are "raised pies"; that is, the pastry casing is "raised." The pastry in this recipe is also used for pork pies. It is my opinion that meat pies will become popular in America due to the high cost of meat. They have been a tradition in England since the Middle Ages.

2 pounds diced lean veal
1 pound diced lean smoked ham
¼ cup chopped parsley
6 tablespoons brandy
6 tablespoons chicken or beef stock
2 tablespoons lemon juice
1 teaspoon salt
¼ teaspoon pepper
1 teaspoon sage
1 teaspoon grated lemon peel

4 cups sifted flour
½ teaspoon salt
½ cup plus 2 tablespoons fat (butter, lard or vegetable shortening)
½ cup water
4 hard-boiled eggs
1 egg yolk, beaten with 1 tablespoon milk or heavy cream
1 tablespoon gelatin
2 cups chicken stock

Toss diced veal and ham with the parsley, brandy, six tablespoons of stock, lemon peel, and seasonings. In a saucepan, bring the fat, water and salt to a boil. Stir in, all at once, the sifted flour, stirring until the mixture leaves the sides of the pan. Remove from fire and continue stirring until it is cool enough to handle. Knead on a floured board until the dough is smooth, cover with a cloth, and let it rest for 30 minutes. Knead again for a few minutes and then roll out ⅔ of the dough ¼-inch thick. Line a buttered 10- × 5- × 4-inch loaf pan.

Spread out half of the meat mixture and arrange the hard boiled eggs on it. Cover with remaining meat. Roll out the remaining dough and drape it over the top of the pie. Moisten edges and crimp together. Make a hole in the center of the top, brush with beaten egg, and bake in a 300° oven for two hours. Meanwhile, soften gelatin in two cups of stock for a few minutes. Stir over low heat until gelatin is dissolved, and pour through a funnel into the opening in the pie. Refrigerate until aspic is set (6 to 8 hours).

The pie should be removed from the refrigerator 30 minutes before serving. To unmold, run a sharp knife around inside edges of pan and dip bottom of pan in hot water. Wipe pan dry, place inverted serving plate over it, and holding pan and plate together firmly, turn over. Rap the plate on table and pie will slide out easily. Turn pie over; cut into ½-inch thick slices. Serves 6 to 8.

CHICKEN AND LEEK PIE

Britons have for centuries hunted various birds for their pots or pies and since the national emblem of Wales is the leek, it's no surprise that the 'Taffies' (the Welsh) have several chicken and leek pies.

4- to 5-pound roasting chicken or stewing fowl
1 large onion, peeled and quartered
1 small celery stalk, include the leaves
10 sprigs parsley and 1 to 2 small bay leaves tied together
¼ teaspoon thyme
1 tablespoon salt
¼ pound cooked, smoked beef tongue cut into ⅛-inch slices

12 medium-sized leeks, including 1 inch of the green stems, split in half and cut across into 1-inch pieces
1 tablespoon finely chopped parsley
1 Rough Puff Pastry recipe (see page 131)
1 egg yolk combined with 1 tablespoon heavy cream
¼ cup heavy cream

Using a heavy, 8-quart pot, combine the chicken or fowl, onion, celery stalk, parsley sprigs, bay leaves, thyme, and salt. Pour cold water to cover the chicken by 1 inch. Bring to boil at high heat and skim off foam and scum. Reduce heat and simmer, partially covered, until the bird is tender. Transfer chicken to plate and strain the stock through fine sieve set over bowl, pressing down hard on the vegetables and herbs with the back of a spoon before discarding them. Pour 2 cups of the stock into a heavy, 2 to 3 quart saucepan and skim the surface of its fat. Add the leeks and bring to a boil. Reduce heat and simmer, partially covered, for 15 minutes or until leeks are tender. Remove the skin from the chicken and cut the meat away from bones. Cut meat into 1-inch pieces and arrange evenly on the bottom of a 1½ quart casserole. Pour the leeks and their stock over the chicken and season with salt. Arrange the slices of tongue side by side over the top but leave a 1-inch space in the center. Sprinkle with chopped parsley.

Preheat oven to 400°. On lightly floured surface, roll out the puff pastry into a rough rectangle about ¼-inch thick. Cut two strips each about 12 inches long and ½-inch wide, from the ends. Lay strips end to end around the rim of a baking dish and press them firmly into place. Moisten slightly with pastry brush and cold water. Drape the remaining pastry over the rolling pin, lift it up, and unfold it over the baking dish. Trim off excess with a small knife, and with the tines of a fork or your fingers, crimp the pastry to secure it to the rim of the dish. Gather scraps of pastry into a ball, reroll and cut into simple leaf and flower shapes. Moisten one side with egg yolk and cream mixture and arrange shapes decoratively on the pie. Then brush the entire pastry surface with remaining egg yolk and cream mixture and cut a 1-inch round hole in center of pie. Bake the pie in the middle of the oven for 1 hour, or until crust is golden brown. Just before serving, heat the ¼ cup of cream to lukewarm and pour it through the hole in the cross. Serves 4 to 6.

CRAB PIE

1½ pounds Rough Puff Pastry (see page 131)
1 pound crab meat
½ pound filleted salmon
1 medium, finely chopped onion
½ cup currants
2 tablespoons peeled grapes
¼ cup bread crumbs
4 tablespoons chopped herbs (sage, dill, tarragon)
¼ teaspoon ground nutmeg
2 tablespoons butter
½ cup white wine

You can use two small soufflé dishes or one 8-inch pie dish. Line with half the pastry. Arrange layers of crab, salmon, onion, currants, grapes, bread crumbs, and herbs. Now season the layers with salt, pepper, and nutmeg. Dot with butter and pour the wine over the dish. Cover with a pastry lid and bake at 375° for 15 to 20 minutes. Serve hot or cold. Serves 4.

SHRIMP PIE

2 tablespoons butter
1 pound small shrimp, peeled, deveined, and boiled 5 minutes
½ pound cooked macaroni
⅓ cup bread crumbs
1 tablespoon butter
½ teaspoon salt
Ground pepper
2 tablespoons finely chopped parsley
2 tablespoons shrimp cocktail sauce
1 teaspoon lemon juice
2 tablespoons flour
1½ cups milk

Melt 2 tablespoons of butter in saucepan. Stir in flour and add milk slowly, stirring with wire whisk to form a smooth sauce. Stir in lemon juice, cocktail sauce, parsley, salt, and pepper. Combine sauce with macaroni and shrimp. Place the mixture in a buttered baking dish. Top with bread crumbs, dot with butter, and place in a 400° oven for 10 minutes. Serves 4.

Breads

GINGERBREAD LEMON PEEL

½ cup boiling water
½ cup shortening
½ cup cooked lemon peel
½ cup brown sugar
½ cup molasses
1 beaten egg
1½ cups sifted flour
½ teaspoon salt
½ teaspoon baking powder
½ teaspoon soda
¾ teaspoon ginger
¾ teaspoon cinnamon

Pour the boiling water over shortening. Add remaining ingredients and beat until smooth. Turn into 8-inch square buttered pan. Bake in oven at 325° for approximately 40 minutes. Cool on rack. Makes 8 servings.

SEMI-SWEET BISHOP'S BREAD

3 eggs
½ cup sugar
1 teaspoon vanilla extract
1½ cups unsifted flour
1 6-ounce package (1 cup) semi-sweet chocolate morsels
1 cup chopped dates
1 cup chopped nuts
1 cup whole candied cherries
½ cup mixed candied fruit
1 teaspoon salt
3 tablespoons brandy

Preheat oven to 325°. In small bowl, beat eggs until thick and lemon-colored (about 5 minutes). Gradually beat in sugar and vanilla extract. In large bowl, combine flour, semi-sweet chocolate morsels, dates, nuts, candied cherries, candied fruit, and salt. Mix well. Fold in egg mixture. Spread in greased and floured 9- × 5- × 3-inch loaf pan. Bake at 325° for one hour. Remove from oven; cool ten minutes. Remove from pan and invert. With toothpick, make 1½-inch deep holes in cake. Slowly pour brandy over the top. Wrap tightly in aluminum foil. Store at room temperature overnight. Slice and serve.

IRISH SODA BREAD

2 cups all-purpose flour
1½ teaspoon baking powder
½ teaspoon baking soda
2 tablespoons sugar
½ teaspoon salt
2 tablespoons butter
1 cup buttermilk
½ cup currants

Teatime

Preheat oven to 375°. Sift the flour, baking powder, soda, salt, and sugar in a deep bowl. Cut the butter into flour mix with pastry blender. Add the buttermilk. Mix into a soft dough. Add currants. On a lightly floured board, knead the dough until smooth. Shape the dough into a flat circular 7-inch loaf, and place on a baking sheet. With small knife, cut a ½-inch deep cross in the center of the round, dividing the top of the loaf into quarters. Bake in oven about 40 minutes at 375°. Cool on wire rack.

FLAPJACKS (OATMEAL PANCAKES)

1½ cups quick-cooking oatmeal
3 tablespoons brown sugar
1½ cups milk

¼ teaspoon salt
2 tablespoons melted butter
½ cup flour
½ teaspoon baking soda

Combine the oatmeal, baking soda, and salt in a mixing bowl. Stir in milk and butter and beat well. Drop the batter onto hot, greased griddle or frying pan. When holes appear all over the surface of the flapjacks, quickly turn them over and brown. Serve immediately with melted butter and maple syrup. Makes 24 flapjacks.

Cakes, Buns, and Biscuits

DUNDEE CAKE

Only shortbread, probably, ranks with Dundee Cake as Scotland's most famous cake or pastry. A good hot cup of tea makes a slice taste all the better.

¾ cup butter, softened
¾ cup sugar
4 eggs
2 cups all-purpose flour
1¼ teaspoons baking powder
¼ teaspoon salt
2 tablespoons finely ground almonds
1 cup seedless golden raisins
1 cup dried currants
6 candied cherries, cut in half
⅓ cup mixed candied fruit peel, chopped
2 tablespoons finely grated orange peel
⅓ cup blanched almonds, split lengthwise into halves

Cream butter and sugar together until light and fluffy. Add 2 eggs, one at a time, beating well after each addition. Mix flour, baking powder, and salt together; blend well. Beat in ½ cup of the flour mixture. Add the remaining eggs, one at a time, alternating with the remaining flour mixture, beating well after each addition. Add ground almonds, currants, raisins, cherries, fruit peel, and grated orange peel; mix well. Butter and flour the bottom and sides of an 8- × 3-inch springboard pan, tipping the pan to spread the flour evenly. Invert the pan and rap it to remove excess flour. Transfer the batter evenly into the pan. Place the split blanched almonds in circles over the top. Bake in preheated 325° oven for 1½ hours or until cake tester comes out clean. Cool 5 minutes in pan, then run spatula around sides of pan, invert, and cool cake thoroughly on wire rack. Makes about 8 to 10 servings.

PEG'S IRISH TEA CAKE

This cake is pleasantly moist and keeps well for several days. Peg says: "It makes a nice little cake."

1 cup strong tea
1½ cups raisins
1 tablespoon brown sugar
1 egg, well beaten
1 cup chopped walnuts
2 cups flour
1 teaspoon baking powder
¼ cup milk

Dissolve brown sugar in tea; steep raisins in mixture overnight. Next day, add well-beaten egg and chopped nuts. Sift flour and baking powder; add to mixture. Add milk and mix well. Bake for 1 hour in 350° oven.

MADEIRA CAKE

½ cup butter
½ cup sugar
4 eggs
2 cups self rising flour
Grated rind of one lemon

2 tablespoons superfine
   sugar
3-inch piece of candied
   lemon peel

Cream the butter with the sugar until light and fluffy. Add 2 eggs, one at a time, beating well after each egg. Add ½ cup of flour and beat thoroughly. Add the remaining eggs, then the flour and lemon rind. Combine thoroughly. Place the batter in a buttered and floured 9- × 5-inch loaf pan. Bake in a 350° oven for 30 minutes. Now sprinkle the sugar on top of the cake and place the strip of lemon peel in the center. Continue to bake for another 30 minutes.

GOOSEBERRY LAYER CAKE

1½ cups self-rising flour
  6 tablespoons butter
  1 large can gooseberries
    or raspberries

¼ cup sugar
½ teaspoon ground nutmeg
Confectioners sugar for
   decoration

Sift the flour into mixing bowl. Add the sugar and nutmeg. Then add the butter in small pieces and work in. Use half of the mixture and put into a greased, 8-inch round cake pan. Drain the gooseberries and place over mixture. Cover with the rest of the mix. Evenly spread the mixture and pat it down. Place in the middle of a 400° oven for 20 to 30 minutes. Then remove the pan for 5 minutes, allowing the shortcake to cook. Put serving plate on top, then turn pan and plate upside down. Remove the pan so that the cake is on the plate. Dust, using sifted confectioners sugar. Use cake knife and cut into wedges. Serve warm with cream. Serves 8.

SALLY LUNN

A Somerset lass at the end of the 19th century used to make and sell these in the fashionable town of Bath. This tea cake is named after her.

4½ cups flour
½ cup softened butter
½ ounce (1 package) yeast
⅛ teaspoon of salt
3 eggs
¼ cup lukewarm water
⅓ cup sugar
½ cup milk

Dissolve the yeast in the warm water. Mix the flour, sugar, and salt in a bowl. Make a well in the middle and put in the eggs, butter, milk, and the made-up yeast mixture. Blend thoroughly. With a mixer, beat at high speed for 2 minutes. If necessary, stir in more flour to make a stiff dough. Cover and put in warm place to rise for 1 hour or until the dough has doubled in size. Then, punch down and knead until smooth. Shape into small round buns and place on a greased baking sheet. Let rise again for 1 hour, or until they have doubled in size. Bake at 325° for 20 to 25 minutes. You can include currants, sultanas, and a little spice to taste. Makes about 18 buns.

BANBURY CAKES

- 2 tablespoons butter, melted
- 3 tablespoons sugar
- ½ cup currants
- 2 tablespoons mixed candied fruit peel, finely chopped
- ¼ teaspoon ground spice
- ½ teaspoon cinnamon
- ⅛ teaspoon ground nutmeg
- 1 plain sweet biscuit, dried in the oven until very crisp and ground into crumbs in blender
- 1½ pound pastry
- Dusting of confectioner's sugar

Combine the melted butter and sugar in a bowl and stir in the currants, peel, spices, and biscuit crumbs. Roll out the pastry on a floured board until ¼-inch thick. Cut into 3½-inch circles. Place one tablespoon of the mixture on each circle of pastry and fold the edges towards the center to seal in the filling. Turn them upside down and flatten a little with a rolling pin. The currants should be just visible below the surface of the dough. Insert an inch-long gash on the surface in the shape of an X. Brush with lightly whipped egg white and dust with sugar. Put on floured baking sheet and bake in 400° oven for 10 to 15 minutes. Makes 12 to 15 cakes.

DEVONSHIRE TEACAKES

- 4½ cups flour
- ¼ cup butter
- ¼ cup sugar
- ½ teaspoon cinnamon
- ½ cup sultanas
- 3 tablespoons milk
- ½ ounce yeast
- Pinch of salt

Mix salt and cinnamon with the flour, rub in butter, and stir in the sugar. Mix well. Warm the milk and dissolve the yeast in it. Now, make a hole in the middle of the flour, pour the milk, and yeast mixture in, and form into a dough. If necessary, add a little more milk. Stand in a warm place for one hour. Knead in the sultanas. Divide the dough into small pieces. Then form into buns and leave to rise for one half-hour. Place in a 425° oven and bake for 15 minutes. Serve hot with butter.

SHREWSBURY TEACAKES

1 cup butter, softened
½ cup confectioners sugar
1 egg, beaten
1 tablespoon caraway seeds
2 cups flour

Take the softened butter and beat it with the sugar until fluffy. Add the beaten egg and caraway seeds. Stir in the flour, adding enough to make a stiff paste, and roll the dough out on floured board. Cut into circles. Bake on a greased baking sheet at 350° for 10 minutes. Serve hot. Ideal spread with raspberry jam and topped with ice cream.

WELSH CAKES

2 cups flour
1 teaspoon baking
  powder
1 teaspoon allspice
¼ teaspoon salt
½ cup sugar

¼ cup butter
¼ cup shortening
1 egg
¼ cup milk
⅓ cup currants

    Sift the flour, baking powder, allspice, salt, and sugar together into a bowl. Cut the butter and shortening into the flour, using a pastry blender or two knives. Stir the egg with the milk. Add the egg mixture to the flour mixture and blend well. Blend in the currants. Gather the dough into a ball. Roll out on a floured board ¼-inch thick. Cut out 2-inch rounds and cook on a very hot oiled frying pan or griddle until well browned. Turn and cook on the other side until brown. Serve warm. Makes 15 to 20.

YORKSHIRE TEACAKES

1½ teaspoons dry yeast
¼ cup lukewarm water
¼ cup lukewarm milk
2 tablespoons sugar

1½ cups flour
¼ teaspoon salt
2 tablespoons
  shortening

    Sprinkle the yeast over the lukewarm water and stir to dissolve. Add the milk and sugar. Sift the flour with the salt into a bowl. Cut in the shortening, using a pastry blender or two knives. Add the flour mixture, ½ cup at a time, to the liquid. Knead in the last amount of flour. Place the dough in an oiled bowl, cover, and set in a warm place until dough doubles in size. Turn dough out onto a floured board and knead a few times. Divide dough into 24 small pieces. Roll each into a small round. Place the teacakes on an oiled baking sheet and prick with a fork. Cover and let the teacakes rise 30 minutes. Bake in a 400° oven for 12 to 15 minutes.

SINGIN' HINNIES (CURRANT CAKES)

These delicious cakes make a sizzling, singing sound as they cook. In Northumberland, where they originated, "hinny" is a term of affection, and Northumberlanders are very fond of their "Singin' Hinnies."

3½ cups unsifted all-purpose flour
1 teaspoon salt
2¼ teaspoons baking powder
¼ cup sugar
½ cup currants
1¼ cups milk
4 tablespoons melted butter
Oil for frying

In mixing bowl, combine flour, salt, baking powder, sugar, and currants. Mix milk and melted butter; stir into dry ingredients. Place dough on floured surface and roll out ¼-inch thick. Cut into 3-inch rounds and prick all over with fork tines. Bake on a hot oiled griddle or skillet until well browned. Turn and brown the other side. Serve warm with butter or split them in half, toast, and butter. (Makes about 2 dozen.)

CHELSEA BUNS

Of all the teatime delicacies, buns seem most closely identified with their native localities. Chelsea buns originated in the borough of Chelsea in London.

BREAD
- 1½ teaspoons dry yeast
- 1 tablespoon lukewarm water
- 1 teaspoon sugar
- ¾ cup lukewarm milk
- 3 cups all purpose flour
- 4 tablespoons butter
- ¼ teaspoon salt
- 2 tablespoons sugar
- 1 egg, lightly beaten

FILLING
- 4 tablespoons butter, softened
- 4 tablespoons sugar
- ¾ cup mixed candied fruits, chopped

GLAZE
- 4 tablespoons powdered sugar
- 1 tablespoon water

Dissolve the yeast in the lukewarm water. Stir in the 1 teaspoon sugar, the milk, and ½ cup flour. Set in warm place for 20 minutes. Now cut the butter into the remaining flour, using a pastry blender or two knives. Mix in salt and 2 tablespoons sugar. Add the egg to the yeast mixture. Add the flour to the yeast mixture ½ cup at a time. Knead in the final amount if the dough becomes too stiff to stir. On a lightly floured board, turn the dough out and knead until smooth and elastic. Do not add any additional flour. Shape dough into a ball and place in an oiled bowl. Cover and let rise until double. Knead the dough a few times on a floured board; then roll into a rectangle. Spread the dough with 4 tablespoons butter.

Teatime

Sprinkle on the sugar and the candied fruits. Roll the dough up tightly as for a jelly roll. Cut into 12 to 14 pieces and form each piece into a ball. Place buns on oiled baking sheet. Cover and let rise 25 minutes. Bake in 400° oven for about 20 minutes. Combine the powdered sugar and water and brush the glaze on the warm buns. Makes 12 to 14.

SHORT CRUST PASTRY
(FOR RICHMOND MAIDS OF HONOUR)

1½ cups all purpose flour
2 tablespoons chilled lard cut into ¼-inch pieces
1 tablespoon sugar
¼ teaspoon salt

6 tablespoons sweet butter, chilled and cut into ¼-inch pieces
3 to 4 tablespoons ice water

Combine the butter, lard, flour, salt, and sugar in a large chilled bowl. With your fingertips, rub the fat and flour together until they look like coarse meal. Make sure the mixture does not become oily. Take 3 tablespoons of ice water and pour over the mixture. Toss lightly and make the dough into a ball. Should the dough crumble, add up to 1 tablespoon more ice water by drops until the dough is firm but fairly soft, so that you can roll it easily. Dust the pastry with a little flour and wrap in wax paper. Refrigerate for 1 hour before using.

RICHMOND MAIDS OF HONOR
(ALMOND TARTS)

These small, delightfully rich cakes were invented at Queen Elizabeth's palace at Richmond to tempt the queen's appetite. It is said that her maids of honor liked them so much that the cakes received their name. The original recipe passed to a baker shop in Richmond, which had the sole rights to make them for many years. You could buy them there until about twenty years ago when the shop was pulled down.

1 pound short crust pastry
1 cup cottage cheese mixed with ¾ cup fresh butter
4 egg yolks beaten with a glass of brandy (cognac) and ¾ cup sugar
1 cup very fine bread crumbs, mixed with ½ cup ground almonds and touch of nutmeg
Juice of 1 lemon and the grated peel of 2 lemons

Preheat oven to 400°. Using pastry brush and two tablespoons of soft butter, coat the inside surfaces of two medium 12-cup muffin tins. Sprinkle 4 tablespoons of flour into the tins, tipping them to coat the bottoms and sides evenly. Then turn the tins over and rap them sharply on a table to remove the excess flour. Line pastry into muffin tins, pushing the pastry firmly into the sides. The pastry shells will be about 1-inch deep and will not fill the cups completely. Work all the other ingredients into the cottage cheese and butter, beating well. Now, ladle about 1 tablespoon of the mixture into each pastry shell filling to within ⅛th inch of the top. Bake at 400° for 10 minutes, or until the filling is golden brown. Remove tarts from tins and cool to room temperature. In some parts of Britain jam is added to the filling and two crossed strips of dough are topped over the tart. Maids of Honor are traditionally served with afternoon tea. Makes about 24 tarts.

TEA WAFERS

½ cup butter
1 cup confectioners sugar
1 teaspoon vanilla
½ cup milk

1¾ cups all purpose flour
Chopped nutmeats or cinnamon and sugar or grated lemon rind

Preheat oven to 325°. Cream butter; then sift and beat in 1 cup confectioners sugar until smooth. Add 1 teaspoon vanilla. Sift, then add flour. Resift and add to the creamed mixture, alternately with milk. Beat until creamy. Lightly butter baking sheet and then chill. Using a spatula, spread only about 2 tablespoons of the mixture over the sheet as thinly and evenly as possible. Sprinkle the dough with the chopped nutmeats or cinnamon and sugar or grated lemon rind. Make sure to press the nuts in so that they stick. Using a sharp knife, mark off the dough in 1½-inch squares. Bake about 5 minutes or until brown. When done, remove from oven and, while hot, quickly cut through the marked squares. Slip a knife under to remove from sheet. The wafers grow crisp as soon as they cool and break easily, so work fast. As soon as they are cool, they must be placed in a tightly covered tin. This will keep them for several weeks. Makes about 100 paper-thin wafers.

SCOTCH SHORTBREAD

1 cup butter
2 cups sifted all-purpose flour
½ cup confectioners sugar
¼ teaspoon salt

Preheat oven to 325°. Blend the dry ingredients into the butter. Pat the stiff dough into an ungreased 9- × 9-inch pan and press edges down. With a fork, pierce through the dough every half inch. Bake 25 to 30 minutes. Cut into squares while warm. Makes about 20 squares.

BRANDY SNAPS

Like wafers, brandy snaps were made as early as the twelfth century. They were sticky and pliable, cooked on one side only, peeled off a flat iron and rolled. They are still very popular today.

2 cups flour
2 teaspoons finely grated lemon peel
½ cup butter
1 cup brown sugar
2 eggs, well beaten
2 teaspoons brandy (cognac)
½ teaspoon ground ginger

Rub the butter into flour. Add eggs, sugar, brandy, ginger, and finely grated lemon peel. Beat until smooth. The batter must be of a soft dropping consistency. Heat a griddle or a very large frying pan so that butter dropped on it sizzles and smokes immediately. Drop batter by the teaspoonful on to the buttered pan, well apart, and allow to spread to the size of saucers (becoming full of holes at the same time). Quickly lift, roll each on a stick, and place on a rack until they are dry and crisp. Serve with whipped cream.

Sweets

TEA-LIME PIE

1 envelope unflavored gelatin
¼ cup cold water
¾ cup boiling water
1 cup heavy cream
Fresh strawberries, optional

1 envelope lime-flavored iced tea mix
1 9-inch prepared graham pie crust, chilled

Sprinkle gelatin on cold water and let soften. Add boiling water and stir until gelatin is dissolved. Cool and chill until consistency of unbeaten egg white. (Do not let it set.) Meanwhile, whip cream until frothy, then slowly add and whip in iced tea mix. Continue whipping until mixture holds soft peaks. Beat in the slightly thickened gelatin. Pour into crust. Refrigerate until set. When ready to serve, garnish with strawberries, if desired. (Makes 6 servings.)

BUTTERSCOTCH PUMPKIN MINCE PIE

1 teaspoon cinnamon
½ teaspoon salt
½ teaspoon ginger
¼ teaspoon nutmeg
1 6-ounce package (1 cup) butterscotch morsels
¼ cup milk
¾ cup canned pumpkin
2 eggs, slightly beaten
1 cup mincemeat
1 unbaked 9-inch pie shell

Preheat oven to 375°. In small bowl, combine cinnamon, salt, ginger, and nutmeg; set aside. Combine over hot (not boiling) water, butterscotch morsels and milk; stir until morsels melt and mixture is smooth. Add pumpkin and mix until smooth. Blend in eggs and spice mixture, stirring vigorously. Spread mincemeat evenly into pie shell. Pour pumpkin mixture over mincemeat. Bake at 375° for 35 to 40 minutes. Cool.

"LOVABLE" PUMPKIN PIE

1 9-inch pastry shell, unbaked
2 cups canned pumpkin
1 cup sugar
½ cup Amaretto di Saronno
¼ teaspoon nutmeg
½ teaspoon each salt, cinnamon, ginger
⅔ cup slivered almonds
1 cup heavy cream
Additional Amaretto di Saronno as needed

Set aside pastry. Combine all other ingredients in bowl of electric mixer; mix at low speed until well blended. Pour filling into pie shell and sprinkle top with slivered almonds. Bake in 450° oven for 15 minutes or until filling is set. Cool and garnish with cream whipped with 2 tablespoons Amaretto.

LADY TIDDLEWINK'S ORANGE TRIFLE

This is your gracious Southern cousin to our traditional English dessert. Absolutely fruity, light, sweet, orangey. The goodness threads through the cake cubes and around the sumptuous combination of pecans, cherries, and raisins. It's a great "mate" with tea.

1½ tablespoons cornstarch
½ cup sugar
1½ cups milk
1½ cups orange juice
3 egg yolks
2 cups orange sections
½ cup candied cherries
¼ cup raisins
3 strips orange peel
½ teaspoon vanilla
½ cup chopped pecans
1 pound cake loaf, cut into cubes (6 cups)
Whipped cream

In medium saucepan, mix cornstarch and sugar. Stir in milk, ½ cup of orange juice, and orange peel strips. Stir over medium heat until mixture thickens and comes to a boil. Beat egg yolks until well mixed and stir in a little of hot mixture. Stir yolk mixture back into saucepan and cook, stirring constantly, until thickened, about 3 to 5 minutes. Do not boil. Remove from heat, discard orange strips, and stir in vanilla. Cool.

In large bowl, combine remaining 1 cup orange juice, orange sections, cherries, pecans, and raisins. Set aside. To assemble trifle, place a layer of cake cubes in bottom of bowl, spoon half of orange section mixture over cake, and spoon half of orange custard over fruit. Repeat layers, cover, and chill until ready to serve. Garnish with whipped cream and additional orange sections. Yields 8 servings.

"TRIFLE WITH LOVE"

1 layer sponge cake
¼ cup Amaretto di Saronno
Tart currant jam
4 egg yolks
¼ cup sugar

Pinch of salt
2 cups scalded milk
1 teaspoon vanilla
1 cup sweetened whipped cream

Line a glass bowl with an inch-thick layer of sponge cake. Moisten with Amaretto and spread thinly with jam. Beat egg yolks lightly in a double-boiler; stir in sugar and salt and gradually add milk. Cook, stirring constantly, until mixture begins to thicken. Remove from heat, add vanilla, and chill, stirring occasionally. Pour over cake and top with whipped cream. Serves 6.

TREACLE TART

1 cup sifted flour
½ teaspoon salt
5 tablespoons butter
2 tablespoons cold water
¾ cup corn syrup
¾ cup molasses

2 eggs yolks
2 cups fresh bread crumbs
Grated rind and juice of lemon
¼ cup superfine sugar

Combine salt and flour; blend in butter. Add enough water to form a dough. Chill dough for 30 minutes. Then, roll out and line 9-inch pie tin. In a wet bowl, stir together syrup, molasses, egg yolks, bread crumbs, grated lemon rind and juice until well blended. Spoon into pastry shell and bake in a 375° oven for 45 minutes. Sprinkle with the sugar and bake another few minutes until browned. Serves 8.

BREAD AND BUTTER PUDDING

10 thin slices of white bread, crusts removed
4 tablespoons butter, softened
1 cup golden raisins or raisins mixed with currants and candied peel

4 eggs
3 tablespoons sugar
1/8 teaspoon nutmeg
1/2 teaspoon cinnamon
2½ cups milk, scalded
½ cup apricot preserves heated

Cut each slice of bread in half diagonally; butter well. Arrange half of the slices, buttered side up, in a shallow buttered baking dish. Add raisins and cover with remaining bread slices. Beat the eggs, sugar, nutmeg, and cinnamon together. Gradually mix in hot milk; pour over the bread. Bake in preheated 350° oven until bread is light brown and custard is set, about 30 minutes. Spread hot pudding with apricot preserves. Serve warm. Serves 6 to 8.

SPOTTED DICK

PASTRY
1½ cups self-rising flour, sifted
1¼ cups fresh bread crumbs
¾ cup chopped beef suet
10 tablespoons cold water

FILLING
2 tablespoons maple syrup
½ cup seedless raisins
½ cup black raisins
3 tablespoons chopped candied orange peel

Combine bread crumbs and sifted flour and blend in suet. Add just enough of the water to form a dough. Roll out into an 8-inch square. Spread with syrup.

Sprinkle with raisins and orange peel and roll up as for a jelly roll. Wrap loosely in foil and seal the two ends. Place in a steamer over boiling water and steam for three hours. Serve with melted butter and cinnamon sugar, or custard sauce. Serves 6.

PLUM PUDDING

A Christmas favorite from Britain's earliest times right down to today. Years ago, cooks would insert sixpenny-pieces into the pudding. This was only a disaster if you swallowed a coin.

3 cups fresh bread crumbs
¾ teaspoon salt
¾ teaspoon cinnamon
½ teaspoon nutmeg
¼ teaspoon ground cloves
¾ cups brown sugar
¾ cups scalded milk
6 beaten eggs
6 ounces ground beef suet
2 cups seeded raisins
½ cup dried currants
¼ cup chopped candied orange peel
¼ cup chopped candied lemon peel
¼ cup chopped candied citron
½ cup chopped apples
¼ cup rum or Amaretto di Saronno

Mix the first 6 ingredients. Add the scalded milk and let the mixture cool. Mix in the beaten eggs and the suet. Add remaining ingredients and blend in evenly. Turn into a buttered mold, cover, and stand on a rack in water in a tightly covered pot. Steam for 4 hours, adding water if necessary. Serve with sauce (recipe follows). Serves 8 to 10.

SAUCE FOR PLUM PUDDING

1 cup brandy
1 cup sherry
1 teaspoon confectioners sugar
4 ounces melted butter
1 teaspoon lemon peel
Sprinkle of nutmeg

Mix the brandy and the sherry. Stir in sugar and lemon peel. In a saucepan, let the butter "just" melt. Slowly stir the melted butter into the sauce mixture. Keep warm over hot water. Stir well and add nutmeg to taste before serving in a ladle and sauce boat. Serves four to six.

CREAM CROWDIE

1 cup oatmeal
1 cup heavy cream, whipped
4 tablespoons sugar
1 teaspoon vanilla extract
2 tablespoons dark rum
1 pint fresh raspberries

Spread oatmeal on a cookie sheet and toast in medium oven for 20 minutes, taking care not to burn it. Cool oatmeal. Add sugar, rum, and vanilla to the whipped cream. Fold in the cooled oatmeal and the berries. Chill thoroughly. Serves 6.

BLACKBERRY AND APPLE PUDDING

6 green cooking apples, peeled, cored, and thinly sliced
2 pounds fresh blackberries
12 tablespoons sugar
½ teaspoon cinnamon
6 tablespoons soft butter
2 beaten eggs
1 cup self-rising flour, sifted with
2 tablespoons cornstarch

Arrange apple slices and berries in a baking dish. Sprinkle with half the sugar and the cinnamon. Separately, cream remaining sugar with the butter until very light. Beat in the eggs and add the flour and cornstarch. Spread mixture over fruit and bake in 375° oven for 40 minutes. Serve with custard sauce or whipped cream. Serves 6.

APPLE CHARLOTTE

As late as the fifteenth century "charlotte and forst" contained chopped pork or veal and was cooked in milk and almonds. In the great kitchens of the eighteenth and nineteenth centuries, however it appeared as a molded dessert more like a pudding or smooth purée filled into a crust or a bed of biscuits.

8 slices bread
½ cup soft butter
8 cups green apples, peeled, cored, and quartered
½ cup sugar
½ teaspoon cinnamon
½ teaspoon ground nutmeg
¼ cup blanched, slivered almonds, toasted

Brush bread with soft butter and lightly brown in a heavy skillet. Cut in strips and line a baking dish, using 6 of the slices. Cook apples with a small amount of water and a little butter until tender. Mash lightly and mix in sugar, cinnamon, and nutmeg. Fill the bread-lined casserole, sprinkle almonds on top, and cover with remaining bread strips. Bake in a 400° oven for 25 minutes. Serve with custard sauce or lightly whipped cream. Serves 6 to 8.

BURNT CREAM

1 quart scalded heavy cream
8 egg yolks
¼ cup sugar
1 tablespoon vanilla extract or 1 vanilla bean
½ cup brown sugar

Beat egg yolks and ¼ cup sugar until thick. Strain the scalded cream and beat slowly into the egg yolks. Add vanilla and pour into a baking dish. Place dish into a shallow pan of water and bake in a 300° oven for one hour. Chill thoroughly until ready to serve. Set dish in a shallow pan filled with crushed ice, sprinkle with brown sugar and place under a very hot broiler until sugar forms a crust. Serves 6 to 8.

SYLLABUB

One British king was so fond of syllabubs that cows were kept in a park near Buckingham Palace so that as he walked there he might have fresh warm milk mixed in a bowl with sweetened wine to quench his thirst. Sometimes spices were used in the wine, and cream substituted for milk. It was often topped with a spoonful of whipped cream. Syllabubs may also be whipped and piled into a dessert glass.

Grated rind and juice of 1 lemon
½ cup sherry
2 tablespoons brandy
½ cup sugar
2 cups very cold heavy cream

Stir together lemon rind, juice, sherry, brandy, and sugar until dissolved. Place in refrigerator for ½ hour. Add cream and beat until thick. Serve in parfait glasses. Serves 4.

STEAMED LEMON PUDDING

4 tablespoons butter
4 tablespoons sugar
3 beaten eggs
1 cup sifted flour
¼ teaspoon salt
½ teaspoon double-acting baking powder

Grated rind and juice of 1 lemon
4 tablespoons apricot preserves
2 tablespoons rum or sherry

Beat butter and sugar until fluffy. Slowly beat in eggs. Fold in flour, salt, baking powder, lemon rind, and juice. Pour mixture into a buttered mold, cover, and place in a steamer. Steam over boiling water for 1¼ hours. Heat preserves with rum or sherry. Unmold pudding and serve with hot apricot sauce. Serves 6.

QUEEN OF PUDDINGS

2 tablespoons butter
2 cups milk
Grated rind of 2 lemons
¼ cup brown sugar
3 egg yolks
½ cup bread crumbs
½ cup raspberry preserves

TOPPING
2 egg whites
Pinch of salt and cream of tartar
½ teaspoon vanilla
½ cup sugar

Heat butter, milk, lemon rind, and brown sugar to simmering point. Strain and cool. Stir in egg yolks and bread crumbs and pour into buttered pie tin. Bake in a 350° oven for 30 minutes. Spread with preserves. Beat remaining ingredients until stiff and spread meringue over pudding. Bake for 15 minutes more. Serves 6.

GOOSEBERRY FOOL

A gooseberry "foule" was, in ancient times, a purée of gooseberries and sugar or honey baked in an earthenware pot and, when cooked, added to an equal portion of thick cream. Today, fools are often made with raspberries or apricots and custard instead of heavy cream.

1 quart gooseberries
½ cup water
1 cup sugar

2 cups heavy cream, whipped

Pick over berries. Remove stem and blossom end, and wash them. Place in a heavy pot with the water and sugar and cook over low heat until tender, stirring occasionally. If necessary, add more sugar. Puree in blender, or strain through food mill and let mixture cool. Carefully fold in whipped cream and chill well for at least two hours. Serves 4.

APPLE DUMPLINGS

2 cups sifted flour
½ teaspoon salt
1 tablespoon sugar
5 ounces butter
1 egg yolk
3 tablespoons cold water
6 large green apples, peeled and cored
6 tablespoons raisins

6 teaspoons chopped candied orange peel
6 tablespoons chopped walnut meats
6 teaspoons brown sugar
3 teaspoons soft butter
1 egg yolk, beaten with 2 tablespoons milk

Combine flour, salt, and sugar and blend well with the butter. Add the egg yolk and enough water to form a dough. Chill dough for ½ hour. Roll out into 6 even squares. Place an apple in the center of each pastry square and divide next 5 ingredients evenly to fill the cavities of the cored apples. Wrap apples in pastry and pinch ends together. Place on buttered cookie sheet, brush with yolk, and milk mixture, and bake in 375° oven for 40 minutes. Serves 4.

LEMON FOAM

2 envelopes lemon-flavored gelatin
2 cups hot water
2 teaspoons lemon juice
Dash of salt
¼ teaspoon grated lemon rind
2 egg whites
Whole strawberries

Dissolve gelatin in hot water. Add lemon juice, lemon rind, and salt. Chill until slightly thickened. Place bowl in container of ice and water; beat gelatin with egg beater until mixture is fluffy and thick. Beat egg whites until soft peaks form, and fold into whipped gelatin. Pour into 6-cup mold. Chill until firm. Serve with whole strawberries. Makes 8 servings.

FRESH FRUIT AND YOGURT

1 8-ounce container vanilla yogurt
Fresh fruit
1 tablespoon Amaretto di Saronno

Combine yogurt and Amaretto. Use as topping for fresh fruit of your choosing—berries, sliced peaches or bananas, seedless grapes, etc.

ORANGE ALMOND TEA TARTS

I remember this tart well! An old girl friend of mine introduced me to this sweet at her home in Ascot.

2 cups unsifted all-purpose flour
¼ cup sugar
1 teaspoon grated orange rind

¾ cup butter or margarine, softened
3 tablespoons orange juice

In large bowl, mix flour, sugar, and orange rind. Cut in butter until mixture resembles coarse meal. Sprinkle orange juice over dough and stir with fork until dough forms a ball. Press 2 tablespoons dough in each of sixteen 2½-inch muffin cups, pressing over the bottom and sides of cups. Bake in 300° oven for 10 minutes while preparing Orange Filling.

ORANGE FILLING
¼ cup soft butter or margarine
1 cup sugar
½ teaspoon vanilla
¼ teaspoon almond extract
1 tablespoon flour

1 teaspoon grated orange rind
3 eggs
⅔ cup orange juice
16 whole blanched almonds

In medium bowl, cream butter, sugar, vanilla, almond extract, and orange rind. Blend in flour. Beat in eggs and orange juice. Pour into partially baked pastry shells that have been baked 10 minutes, and place one almond in the center of each tart. Bake 30 minutes longer in 350° oven until knife inserted in center of filling comes out clean. Cool completely and remove from muffin cups. Yields 16 tarts.

LEMON TEA YOGURT FROST

2 1.8-ounce envelopes lemon-flavored iced tea mix
2 8-ounce containers plain yogurt
1 6-ounce container frozen lemonade concentrate
2 eggs
½ cup sugar
1 29-ounce can pear halves
1 envelope plain gelatin
1 cup whipped cream
Fresh mint for garnish

Combine iced tea mix, yogurt, undiluted lemonade, eggs, and sugar. Beat until smooth. Drain pear halves, reserving syrup. Chill pears. Combine ¾ cup pear syrup and gelatin. Stir over low heat until dissolved. Combine with yogurt mixture. Chill until slightly thickened. Fold in whipped cream. Turn into 9- × 5-inch loaf pan. Freeze until firm, 4 hours or longer. Makes about 1¾ quarts.

To serve, mound scoops of Lemon Tea Yogurt Frost in crystal compote. Arrange chilled pear halves around edge. Garnish with fresh mint. **Note:** if preferred, use 2 tablespoons unsweetened lemon-flavored instant tea. Increase sugar to 1 cup.

Recipe for Tea Leaf Reading

1 Tea Leaf reader
1 Person with a question
1 Shallow white tea cup, narrow at the bottom and wide at the top

1 Teaspoon large leaf tea
Boiling water

    The tea leaf reader makes a cup of tea for the person with a question, who drinks the tea as he concentrates on his question. The tea drinker should leave enough tea in the bottom of the cup to cover the tea leaves. Then, the tea drinker picks up the cup by the handle and "swirls" the tea three times to his left, and turns the cup over slowly, letting it drain. The tea leaf reader turns the cup right side up. Begin reading just to the left of the handle and proceed, turning the cup as you go. Be sure to concentrate on the person asking the question as you continue reading to the left around the cup. The first impression you receive is the answer to the question. The handle represents the person asking the question and his home.

    The further the symbol is from the handle, the more distant the symbol is from the asker. Symbols close to the handle show the immediate future. Symbols near the rim of the cup are further in the future. Symbols on the bottom of the cup represent the distant future.

    It will take a lot of practice and a lot of staring into tea leaves before they begin to make pictures for you. It is rather like trying to see pictures in the embers of a fire or in clouds moving through the sky.

A tree may be interpreted as growth: of a business, a plan, etc. Bridges may mean new starts, or going from one way of thinking to another. Leaves mean changes for the better. Anchors mean stability. Crowns, a reward or distinction.

These symbols bring bad luck with them: coffins, crosses, snakes, rats, swords, guns, hourglasses, monkeys, owls, cats, ravens, and church steeples.

A cat may be interpreted as treachery from an unsuspected source. A coffin means death. An hourglass can mean that time is running out. Swords or guns indicate danger.

Other common symbols are books (an insight), ladders (gradual advancement), cows (financial gain), clouds (doubts), rings (marriage), eggs (luck changes for the better), and initials (these are of significant people in the asker's life).

A line of tea leaves around the cup from the handle and back means a quick trip and return home. Breaks in this line can mean obstacles or stops. If the line is unfinished, the asker will not return home. If the leaves are muddled or cloudy, it is said to be due to the asker's state of mind.

Tea leaves must be read keeping in mind the question which you are asked. Any symbols you see must be interpreted in the context of the asker's life.

The best part of tea leaf reading is that it's okay to read your own! *Go to it and have a lark!*

We are at the end—
But do not be surprised
If in my travels,
I stop by for a "spot of tea"
With thee!

Conversion Tables

LIQUID MEASURES

American
standard cup

Metric Equivalent
(approximately)

1 cup	= ½ pint = 8 fl. oz.	= 2,37 dl (deciliter)
1 (tbs.) tablespoon	= ½ fl. oz. (fluid ounce)	= 1,5 cl (centiliter)
1 (tsp.) teaspoon	= ⅙ fl. oz.	= 0,5 cl
1 pint	= 16 fl. oz.	= 4,73 dl
1 quart	= 2 pints	= 9,46 dl

British
standard cup

Metric Equivalent
(approximately)

1 cup	= ½ pint = 10 fl. oz.	= 2,8 dl
1 tbs.	= 0,55 fl. oz.	= 1,77 cl
1 tsp.	= ⅕ fl. oz.	= 0,6 cl
1 pint	= 20 fl. oz.	= 5,7 dl
1 quart	= 2 pints	= 1,1 l (liter)

1 cup = 16 tablespoons
1 tablespoons = 3 teaspoons

1 l (liter) = 10 dl (deciliter) = 100 cl (centiliter)

SOLID MEASURES

American/British   **Metric Equivalent (approximately)**

American/British		Metric Equivalent
1 lb. (pound)	= 16 oz. (ounces)	= 453 g (gram)
	1 oz.	= 28 g
2.2 lbs		= 1000 g = 1 kg (kilogram)
	3½ oz.	= 100 g

OVEN TEMPERATURES

Centigrade	Fahrenheit	
up to 105° C	up to 225° F	cool
105–135° C	225–275° F	very slow
135–160° C	275–325° F	slow
175–190° C	350–375° F	moderate
215–230° C	400–450° F	hot
230–260° C	450–500° F	very hot
260° C	500° F	extremely hot